The American
Economy
A Student Study Guide

The American
Economy

A Student Study Guide

Wade L. Thomas and Robert B. Carson

M.E.Sharpe
Armonk, New York
London, England

Library of Congress Cataloging-in-Publication Data

Thomas, Wade L.
  The American economy : a student study guide / Wade L. Thomas, Robert B. Carson.
     p. cm.
  A student study guide to accompany the principle work, 'The American economy : how it works
and how it doesn't'.
  ISBN 978-0-7656-0759-1 (pbk. : alk. paper)
  1. United States--Economic policy—Examinations—Study guides. 2. United States—Economic
conditions—Examinations—Study guides. I. Carson, Robert Barry, 1934– II. Thomas, Wade L.
American economy : how it works and how it doesn't. III. Title.

  HC103.T475 2011
  330.973—dc22
          2011012002

Printed in the United States of America

The paper used in this publication meets the minimum requirements of
American National Standard for Information Sciences
Permanence of Paper for Printed Library Materials,
ANSI Z 39.48-1984.

IBT (p)   10   9   8   7   6   5   4   3   2   1

Contents

Preface

This *Study Guide* is designed to accompany *The American Economy: How It Works and How It Doesn't,* by Wade L. Thomas and Robert B. Carson. Each *Study Guide* chapter corresponds to one of the seventeen chapters in the text. Every *Study Guide* chapter includes:

1. a list of key terms, for which the definitions are readily found in the main text
2. a summary of the material presented in the next chapter
3. a self examination containing true/false, multiple choice, and problems and thought questions
4. answers to the true/false, multiple choice, and problems and thought questions.

HOW TO USE THE STUDY GUIDE

Before you read a chapter in the textbook, you should inspect the chapter outline and page through the chapter to acquire a general understanding of its flow, highlights, and key terms. Read the chapter, attempt to define the key terms at the end of the chapter, and do the end-of-chapter questions and exercises.

Now review the key terms and chapter summary in the *Study Guide.* If you encounter unfamiliar terms or concepts, find the sections of the text you should reread. When you are comfortable with the key terms and the chapter summary, begin the self examination. You will find questions ranging from simple to complex. If many of the questions seem extremely difficult, however, do not try to guess the correct answer—reread the text! When you have completed the self examination, check your responses using the answer section. Review the questions you missed and attempt to determine the reasoning underlying the correct answers.

The *Study Guide* probably will not reduce the amount of time that you spend studying economics. However, it can help you study more effectively and make learning economics a more rewarding experience.

W.L.T.
R.B.C.

Part 1

Conceptual Foundations

Chapter 1

Toward a Twenty-First Century Economic Agenda: Goals and Possibilities

KEY TERMS

Scarcity
Opportunity cost
Productivity
Law of increasing cost
Economic agenda
Positive economics
Production possibilities curve
Normative economies
Inductive method
Deductive method

Traditional economies
Market economies
Command economies
Microeconomics
Macroeconomics
Capital goods
Consumer goods
Factors of production
Ceteris paribus

CHAPTER SUMMARY

1. The social science of economics exists because the economic resources required to satisfy unlimited human wants are scarce. Because of these scarcities, choices must be made between alternative economic activities.

2. Economic inquiries and models are grounded in the use of logical methods. Economic reasoning must be carefully formulated to avoid erroneous arguments or fallacies.

3. Economics entails reliance upon scientific methods and extols objective inquiry. Nevertheless, economics also incorporates values and prescribes policies to further those values. Laissez-faire economics prescribes no or limited government intervention in the economy. Interventionist views suggest that economic performance can be improved through government policies.

4. A set of economic goals provides the criteria upon which to assess economic performance.

5. Because of scarcity, society has to choose what to produce and how much to allow. The situation is graphically depicted in the production-possibilities curve. The curve shows the tradeoff between two goods (opportunity cost). The model can also be used to illustrate unemployment, underemployment, and economic growth.

6. Numerous items can be placed on the economic agenda for today and for the next century. The central agenda item, upon which the achievement of nearly all other economic goals is contingent, is to sustain economic growth. Sustaining economic growth depends largely upon how society addresses the tradeoff between capital and consumer goods.

7. Economic planning and policy formulation take place in all economies. The process involves applying economic reasoning to help society solve problems that usually have their source in the scarce resource versus unlimited wants dilemma.

SELF EXAMINATION

True/False

1. The discipline of economics and what economists do are well defined.
2. The basic economic problem is that resources are scarce and human wants are unlimited.
3. The inductive method begins with a hypothesis and applies facts for verification.
4. The assumption of *ceteris paribus* means using a model that involves a hypothetical catering service that delivers all outputs via a medium-sized bus.
5. Positive economics is the interpretation of economic facts to arrive at goals which are a reflection of individual value judgments.
6. An equitable distribution of income means that the distribution is fair.
7. Economic resources include land, labor, capital, and managerial skill.
8. Profit is the factor payment to labor.

9. Traditional economies are distinguished from modern economies by the traditional economies' reliance upon markets to answer the fundamental economic questions.

10. The production-possibilities curve shows the maximum combinations of two goods that can be produced with fixed resources and the existing level of technology.

Answer the next three questions using the following production-possibilities data.

Product	Alternatives				
	A	B	C	D	E
Housing (thousands of units)	32	26	19	10	0
Food (millions of tons)	0	10	20	30	40

11. The production-possibilities data reveal that increasing food production entails a constant sacrifice in units of housing.

12. The inverse relationship between the production data of food and housing demonstrates the principle of opportunity cost.

13. Moving from production alternative A to production alternative B means that 10 million tons of food are gained by sacrificing 6,000 housing units.

Multiple Choice

1. Economic choices must be made because:
   a. resources are unlimited and human wants are malleable
   b. resources are limited and human wants are unlimited
   c. political choices are not permitted
   d. political choice mechanisms have failed

2. A theory is:
   a. something that describes reality in minute detail
   b. a half-baked scheme of some kind
   c. a logical method
   d. a generalization of real-world circumstances
   e. a small Greek apple tree

3. Microeconomics differs from macroeconomics in that:
   a. the former is concerned with the entire economy while the latter focuses upon the activities of individual units in the economy
   b. studying the latter before the former induces confusion about the subject
   c. the former deals with policy and the latter strictly with the facts
   d. the former is concerned with consumer behavior, individual firms, market structures, and specific economic problems, while the latter studies the operation of the entire economy
   e. no significant difference can be discerned

4. Some economic theories predict that redistributing income from the rich to the poor will reduce work effort, capital investment, and output. This is known as:
   a. selfishness
   b. the positive-normative dichotomy
   c. the micro-macro fallacy
   d. the efficiency-equity tradeoff
   e. the "I earn, you yearn" maxim

5. If Melinda May works as a crane operator for a construction company, which of the following factor payments would she receive for the labor?
   a. Profits
   b. Interest
   c. Rent
   d. Wages
   e. Public assistance

6. Which of the following characteristics apply to traditional economies?
   a. A strong religious influence
   b. Hierarchical social classes
   c. Feudal manors
   d. Reciprocal responsibilities between serfs and lords
   e. All of the above

Answer the next three questions by relying upon the following production-possibilities data:

Product	Alternatives				
	A	B	C	D	E
Housing (thousands of units)	32	26	19	10	0
Food (millions of tons)	0	10	20	30	40

7. If the economy is currently operating at alternative C, the cost of 10 million more tons of food is:
   a. 7,000 housing units
   b. 9,000 housing units
   c. 9/10 of a housing unit
   d. impossible to determine with the data given

8. These production-possibilities data will graph as:
   a. a curve that is negatively sloped and concave to the origin
   b. a curve that is positively sloped and convex to the origin
   c. a straight, down-sloping line
   d. a curve that is negatively sloped and convex to the origin

9. If the economy is currently at alternative C, the cost of an additional 7,000 housing units is:
    a. zero—it's free
    b. 9,000 tons of food
    c. 10 million tons of food
    d. all 40 million tons of food

10. The loss of jobs in the lumber industry due to stricter environmental rules affecting timber cutting is an example of:
    a. opportunity cost
    b. the law of increasing costs
    c. *ceteris paribus*
    d. factor payments
    e. regulatory triumph over bad business practices

ANSWERS TO SELF EXAMINATION

True/False

1. T
2. T
3. F
4. F
5. F
6. T
7. T
8. F
9. F
10. T
11. F
12. T
13. T

Multiple Choice

1. B
2. D
3. D
4. D
5. D
6. E
7. B
8. A
9. C
10. A

Chapter 2

The Market Economy: Pure and Simple

KEY TERMS

Market

Demand (and Demand schedule)

Law of demand

Utility

Diminishing marginal utility

Reservation price

Income effect

Substitution effect

Supply (and Supply schedule)

Law of supply

Equilibrium

Changes in demand

Determinants of demand

Determinants of supply

Price elasticity

Pricetaker

Pricemaker

Market imperfections

Economies of scale

Market failures

Public goods

Externalities (or Spillovers)

CHAPTER SUMMARY

1. The buying and selling of commodities is the beginning point of the economist's study of human behavior and institutions. These activities certainly predate capitalism but with the rise of capitalist, free-market philosophy after Adam Smith's *Wealth of Nations* (1776), the rules for and the workings of the market were systematically articulated.

2. Central to the working of a market economy is the free interaction of the forces of demand and supply in determining the price and output of specific goods. The demand schedule for a commodity ordinarily reflects the buyers' willingness to purchase more at lower prices and less at higher prices (an inverse relationship between price and quantity demanded). The supply schedule for a particular product reflects the sellers' willingness to produce and sell more goods at higher prices and less at lower prices (a direct relationship between price and quantity supplied). The interplay of the forces of demand and supply will eventually establish in the market an equilibrium price and equilibrium level of output at which neither a shortage nor a surplus of goods exists. The demand schedule, the supply schedule, and equilibrium may be illustrated and analyzed graphically.

3. The market is always a dynamic and changing mechanism. A variety of forces are ever at work determining the demand and supply schedules of any particular good. Changes in these determinants may produce changes (increases or decreases) in demand or supply or both which will, in turn, produce new equilibrium levels of price and quantity.

4. While, in theory at least, a market-driven economy will work through the forces of competition to provide the goods consumers want, to keep prices and costs as low as possible, to encourage efficiency, to distribute income and output according to resource sellers' contributions and to encourage economic growth, market economies do suffer "real world" shortcomings: market imperfections and market failures. Excessive *monopoly power, inadequate knowledge* of products and prices, the failure to produce needed *public goods,* the failure to calculate *externalities* and the use of *common property resources* as well as the inability of the market to deal with problems of *dynamic instability* and certain *ethical and political objectives* of the society frequently require the larger society to intervene in markets to produce certain socially desired objectives. Thus, government interference in markets, although opposed in market theory, is a fact of life in the real-world operation of markets.

SELF EXAMINATION

True/False

1. A market is a system that allocates products and resources through a command-and-control government system.
2. According to the theories advanced by Adam Smith in his *Wealth of Nations* (1776), the first and most important characteristic of a market economy is the right of citizens within that economy to acquire and hold property.
3. Modern "classical economists" and "interventionists" agree that the exercise of monopoly power will

disrupt markets and produce undesirable economic and social outcomes for the larger society.

4. The law of demand holds that the quantity of a commodity demanded by consumers is *directly* related to the price of that commodity.

5. If price and quantity demanded are inversely related, the demand schedule for any commodity is represented on a graph as "down-sloping to the right."

6. The law of supply holds that price and quantity supplied are directly related.

7. The supply curve slopes upward to the right because at higher prices consumers will buy fewer goods.

8. When government sets a legal price above the market equilibrium price, the result will be to produce a shortage of the affected commodity.

9. A rightward shift of the demand curve would be the expected outcome of a decline in demand resulting from lower consumer incomes.

10. Golf balls and tennis racquets are good examples of complementary goods.

11. A rightward shift in the supply curve of product A indicates an increase in supply such as would result from a rise in resource prices used in the production of product A.

12. If government were to pay subsidies to the producers of product X, we could reasonably assume that this will encourage X's production and a shift of X's supply curve to the right.

13. If a 50 percent price reduction leads to a 25 percent increase in sales of a particular item, we can conclude that the demand for this item over the affected price range is inelastic.

14. The principal determinant of a commodity's elasticity of supply is the number of substitutes that exist for that commodity.

15. The market period, the short run, and the long run refer to the periods of time a supplier has to adjust its output to given changes in price.

16. Natural monopolies are usually justified on the grounds that they can exploit economies of scale to the extent that regulation of price and output are a better social option than maintaining competition.

17. If buyers do not possess adequate market knowledge of prices and the quality of available goods, this may lead to a market imperfection in which the market is unable to provide the efficient allocation of resources that would otherwise be expected.

18. The Great Lakes are an example of a common property resource.

19. Higher consumers' incomes will increase the demand for a normal good.

20. The supply curve shows the amounts that consumers are willing and able to purchase at various prices.

Multiple Choice

1. Which of the following was *not* advocated by Adam Smith in his *Wealth of Nations* (1776)?
    a. Firms should operate as pricemakers
    b. Private property
    c. Competition
    d. A minimal role for government
    e. Freedom of economic choice

2. The concept of diminishing marginal utility is evidenced in:
    a. the fact that demand curve slopes down to the right
    b. the fact that we are inclined to buy more of a product if its price declines
    c. the fact we generally obtain less satisfaction from additional units of a commodity we buy
    d. all of the above
    e. none of the above

3. The increase of a consumer's buying power as the result of a decline in prices is called:
    a. the substitution effect
    b. the law of diminishing marginal utility
    c. the law of supply
    d. the income effect
    e. none of the above

4. At any price below the equilibrium price we should reasonably expect:
    a. shortages to exist
    b. a surplus to exist
    c. sellers to be willing to supply greater amounts of the commodity than at equilibrium
    d. all of the above
    e. none of the above

5. Which of the following will cause the demand for automobiles to increase?
    a. A rise in the price of gasoline
    b. A fall in consumer incomes
    c. A decline in the price of steel
    d. Increased number of persons twenty- to forty-years old
    e. All of the above

6. A decrease in the demand for wool sweaters could be explained by:
    a. the expectation that sweater prices will rise in the future
    b. an increase in the overseas sales of wool sweaters
    c. a decline in the price of wool
    d. a decline in the price of cotton sweaters
    e. a rise in the number of sweater buyers

7. Among the principal non-price determinants of the supply of a given commodity are all of the following except:
   a. resources used in producing the commodity
   b. incomes of consumers
   c. the number of suppliers of the product
   d. changes in technology used to produce the product
   e. expectations about the future price of the product

8. A rise in the equilibrium price and a lower equilibrium output of commodity X is consistent with:
   a. an increase in demand and no change in supply of X
   b. a decrease in demand and no change in supply of X
   c. an increase in supply and no change in demand of X
   d. a decrease in supply and no change in demand of X

9. Which of the following goods is the best example of a good for which demand is ordinarily highly price inelastic?
   a. Hamburger
   b. Movie theater tickets
   c. DVD rentals
   d. Houses
   e. Salt

10. Which of the following is an example of a market failure?
    a. A firm is able to suppress its competition and exercise monopoly power
    b. Buyers suffer from inadequate product and price information
    c. Certain public goods (highways, for instance) are not built because there is no way to build and sell them at a profit
    d. All of the above
    e. None of the above

Answer the next four questions using the following data:

Price	Quantity Demanded	Quantity Supplied
$.55	500	800
.50	550	700
.45	600	600
.40	650	500
.35	700	400

11. The equilibrium quantity is:
    a. 500
    b. 550
    c. 600
    d. 650
    e. 400

12. A price of $.40 will:
    a. create a shortage of 150 units
    b. create a surplus of 150 units
    c. be the equilibrium price
    d. be sustainable if the product is taxed

13. A surplus of 300 units will occur at:
    a. the equilibrium price
    b. the price of $.55
    c. a price of $.35
    d. a price not shown in the data set

14. Assume that demand decreases so that the quantities demanded are all reduced by 150 units at each price in the given set of prices. The new equilibrium price will be:
    a. $.35
    b. $.40
    c. $.45
    d. $.50

15. Which of the following statements is consistent with the law of demand?
    a. No matter the price, you must buy it
    b. The price of a product rises and consumers buy less
    c. The quantity of a product supplied rises as the price increases
    d. A rat is trained to behave like its human handlers in order to verify an obscure economic proposition
    e. Production costs remain constant as output is increased

16. The iPhone and a Blackberry are likely:
    a. inferior goods
    b. price inelastic goods
    c. competing goods
    d. produced by the government.

Problems and Thought Questions

1. Given the following price and demand and supply data, answer the questions:

Price	Quantity Demanded	Quantity Supplied
$10	50	300
8	100	250
6	200	200
4	250	100
2	300	50

   a. What will be the equilibrium price and quantity?
   b. If government were to set the legal price at $8, what would be the effect?

c. What would be the effect if government set the legal price at $4?

2. Draw a supply and demand schedule using the data in the first problem. Explain and show the effect of each of the following developments upon equilibrium price and quantity:
   a. There is a general increase in consumer real incomes and commodity X is an ordinary good
   b. The wage rate of labor used in producing X rises
   c. The price of complementary good Y rises
   d. The price of substitute good Z falls

ANSWERS TO SELF EXAMINATION

True/False

1. F
2. T
3. T
4. F
5. T
6. T
7. F
8. F
9. F
10. F
11. F
12. T
13. T
14. F
15. T
16. T
17. T
18. T
19. T
20. F

Multiple Choice

1. A
2. D
3. D
4. A
5. D
6. D
7. B
8. D
9. E
10. C
11. C
12. A
13. B
14. B
15. B
16. C

Problems and Thought Questions

1.
   a. $6 and 200 units
   b. 150 unit surplus
   c. 150 unit shortage

2.
   a. The demand curve shifts to the right; equilibrium price and quantity increase.
   b. The supply curve shifts to the left; equilibrium price rises and equilibrium quantity falls.
   c. The demand curve shifts to the left; equilibrium price and quantity fall.
   d. Same as c.

Chapter 3

Government in the Economy: The Limits of Intervention

KEY TERMS

Benefit-cost analysis   Support prices
MSB = MSC   Price ceilings
Parity price   Black or
Price floors   underground markets
Target pricing

CHAPTER SUMMARY

1. The market system's ability to produce efficient and socially desirable outcomes can be compromised by the existence of market imperfections and market failures. If these are problems of sufficient magnitude, government intervention may be necessary. Government's role in the economy is also justified by the pursuit of economic stabilization and rationalized for ethical and political reasons.

2. The range of tools available to government to correct the shortcomings of markets is extensive. They include laws to counter anticompetitive behavior (antitrust laws), independent regulatory commissions, product disclosure laws, subsidies, taxes, government ownership of certain enterprises, selective use of price and output controls, employment training and development policies, fiscal policy, monetary policy, income redistribution efforts, and many other lesser interventions.

3. Ideally government intervention should be undertaken efficiently. The level of intervention should be determined through analysis of the social benefits and costs. Government intervention should be undertaken to the point where the last unit of intervention adds as much to social benefits as it adds to social costs; MSB = MSC.

4. Although the economic grounds for government intervention are based upon correcting the shortcomings of a private system of market, government actions are subject to problems, too. Difficulties with bureaucracy, interest group pressures, limited knowledge and expertise, unintended consequences, policy delays, tradeoffs between short-run and long-run benefits and costs, external costs caused by government, and conflicting social values are among the readily identifiable shortcomings that can beset government intervention.

5. Three areas of market intervention—agricultural pricing, minimum wage laws, and price controls—provide some insight into the causes for, and practical limits of, government efforts to improve on certain markets. In all of these cases, it can be demonstrated that government intervention produces inefficiency and resource misallocations. However, the withdrawal of such intervention, while perhaps producing greater efficiency, raises equity issues and political questions that may dominate efficiency considerations.

SELF EXAMINATION

True/False

1. One effect of the price controls laid on heating oil and gasoline in the 1970s was to increase American output of petroleum products.
2. It is a general rule of thumb among most economists that if efficient production and distribution conditions are obtained, then an equitable distribution of income always results.
3. To a considerable degree, the economic logic on behalf of efficiency considerations loses out in a democratic society to the political objectives established by a voting majority.
4. Vilfredo Pareto's vision of market optimality rested on the assumption that a high degree of government intervention was in order.
5. Market advocates believe that proper economic conduct results from individuals acting selfishly, while interventionists believe that social welfare is a greater goal then individual self-interest.
6. In determining how much of a certain public good

to provide for the community, cost-benefit analysis holds that additional units should be added up to the point where the marginal social cost of the last unit is equal to its marginal social benefit.

7. Where the marginal social cost of a particular public project (such as the building of a sewerage system) equals the marginal social benefit, there is always a level of provision of that public good that supplies the community with the greatest total benefit.

8. Just as private firms seeking to maximize profits may cause high external costs for the larger community, so also may government intervention be the source of external costs.

9. The revelations of environmental damage caused by U.S. atomic energy plants at Hanford, Washington, and Tom's River, Tennessee are evidence that government operations may also produce high external costs.

10. Most farmers believe that government should cease its efforts to maintain price floors in American agriculture.

11. An effective minimum wage law will reduce the quantity of labor demanded.

12. As a rule, labor unions oppose minimum wage legislation because raising the floor for wages for all workers makes it more difficult to raise the wages of skilled union workers.

13. Rent controls are an example of legal price ceilings, and minimum wage laws are an example of price floors.

14. New York City introduced rent controls during World War II because with the growth of an 11-million-person armed force, the demand for housing in the city fell and landlords were in danger of going bankrupt.

15. When a price ceiling is introduced it is usually because government or the public, or both, believe that the existing price is "too high."

16. Antitrust law is a policy response to externalities.

17. When informational inadequacies exist, the best thing to do is to resort to public ownership.

18. Taxes and transfers can be used to correct for income inequities.

19. "Interventionists" prefer to rely upon markets to manage economic problems.

20. When the market functions perfectly, society's marginal benefits and marginal costs are equalized.

21. Benefit-cost analysis can be used to determine the optimal level of government intervention.

Multiple Choice

1. The U.S. government's actions since 1973 to keep energy prices artificially low have generally had the effect of:
   a. lowering U.S. energy production
   b. increasing consumer use of energy

   c. increasing U.S. dependence on non-American sources of energy
   d. all of the above
   e. none of the above

2. An example of an attempt to "control microeconomic instabilities" would be evident in:
   a. fiscal policy activities
   b. taxation or illegalization of undesirable goods
   c. our agricultural policy
   d. all of the above
   e. none of the above

Answer the next four questions based upon the following diagram.

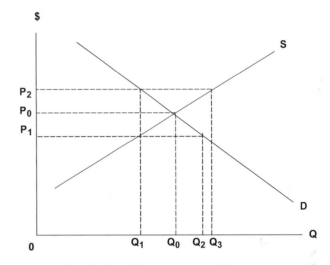

3. A price floor is best represented by:
   a. P_0
   b. P_1
   c. P_2
   d. Q_0

4. A price ceiling is best represented by:
   a. P_0
   b. P_1
   c. P_2
   d. Q_0

5. The quantity Q_1Q_3:
   a. is a surplus arising at the equilibrium price of P_0
   b. is a surplus arising from the floor price of P_2

6. A rent control law that produces a housing shortage in the amount of Q_1Q_2 units can be represented by:
   a. P_0
   b. P_1
   c. P_2
   d. none of the above

7. According to the assumptions of cost-benefit analysis:
   a. the optimal output of any good is where marginal cost is lowest

b. the optimal output of any good is where marginal benefits are lowest

c. the optimal output of any good is where marginal benefit = marginal costs

d. all of the above

e. none of the above

Answer the next three questions based on this chart giving four options for a community that plans to build a new sewerage system, showing the associated costs and benefits of each option. The options are arranged from A to D according to the increased extensiveness of the resulting sewer system.

Plans	Total Cost (in millions of dollars)	Total Benefits (in millions of dollars)
A	10	15
B	25	50
C	50	75
D	100	100

8. Which plan will render the greatest total benefits?

9. Which plan provides the least total benefits in excess of costs?

10. Using MSB = MSC analysis, which plan is the most desirable?

11. The direct economic effect of an effective minimum wage law is most likely to be:

a. a decrease in everyone's money wages

b. the same as any effort to establish a price floor

c. a general increase in hiring by employers

d. a loss of jobs among the lowest skilled workers

e. a general decline in consumer prices

12. Opponents of minimum wage laws would likely argue all of the following except:

a. a minimum wage, while costly, raises overall real wage rates

b. the minimum wage causes unemployment

c. the minimum wage raises product prices

d. the minimum wage penalizes those least able to sustain themselves through employment

13. The term "black market" describes:

a. markets in which illegal goods are sold

b. markets in which sellers seek to sell below the legally established minimum price

c. markets in which illegal goods are sold at higher than legal prices

d. illegal markets that emerge as the result of government imposing effective price ceilings

14. Some accepted reasons for government intervention in the economy are:

a. market imperfections

b. market failures

c. ethical and political contradictions

d. instability

e. all of the above

15. Which of the following have been associated with agricultural policy?

a. Acreage allotments

b. The food for peace program

c. Reducing land under cultivation to improve the environment

d. Food stamps

e. All of the above

Problems and Thought Questions

1. Given the following graph, illustrating the labor market:

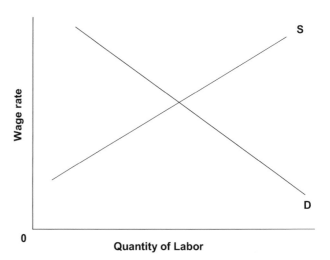

Forecast the impact of imposing an effective minimum wage by marking up the graph. Give and explain your markings.

2. Given the following graph, showing the supply and demand for petroleum:

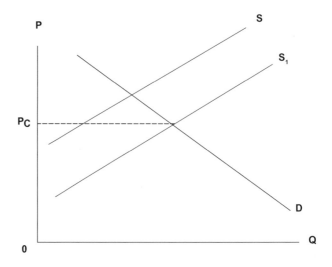

Explain the effect of a government decision to legally set the price at P_C even though there has been a decline in supply from S to S_1. Mark up the graph and explain your markings.

ANSWERS TO SELF EXAMINATION

True/False

1. F
2. F
3. T
4. F
5. T
6. T
7. F
8. T
9. T
10. F
11. T
12. F
13. T
14. F
15. T
16. F
17. F
18. T
19. F
20. T
21. T

Multiple Choice

1. D
2. C
3. C
4. B
5. B
6. B
7. C
8. D
9. D
10. C
11. D
12. A
13. D
14. E
15. E

Problems and Thought Questions

1. An effective minimum wage may be shown as a horizontal wage rate line cutting the supply and demand curves above the present equilibrium point. The result will be to produce a surplus of labor (unemployment) as quantity of labor demand decreases and quantity supplied increases.

2. The effect of this legal maximum price will be to cause a shortage because quantity demanded at the legal price exceeds the quantity supplied.

Chapter 4

The Historical Foundation of American Economic Institutions and Ideas

KEY TERMS

Mercantilism
Trusts
Excess capacity
Progressivism
Durable goods
Nondurable goods
The Great Depression
Business cycles

The New Deal
The New Economics
Multinational business
Discretionary spending
Capital goods
Consumer goods
Stagflation

CHAPTER SUMMARY

1. This chapter is intended to provide a general picture of the contemporary American economy. The contemporary picture, however, is presented in historical relief.

2. Turning to a historical overview of the economy, American economic development has been both unique and remarkable. In successive waves of economic transformation, the United States evolved from a predominantly rural-agrarian organization to an industrial, and most recently, to a structure that emphasizes knowledge services and innovation.

3. A variety of themes may be examined in this process of economic transformation but, for our purposes, perhaps the most interesting has been the evolution, elaboration, and adoption of our "mixed economic system." Despite much rhetorical and theoretical emphasis upon a market economic order, Americans have long employed a pragmatic mix of government and market operations. In this century, the expansion of government in the economy, largely prompted in reaction to cyclical downturns, has been most prominent in the Progressive Era (1900–1920), the Great Depression and World War II (1932–1945), and the Kennedy-Johnson years (1960–1968).

4. The final forty years of the twentieth century are dominated by economic prosperity, but not without

difficult and sometimes surprising interruptions. The successes of the U.S. economy and the perceived improvement in macroeconomic management to counter the business cycle have fostered confidence in sustained expansions. Nonetheless, the economy's resiliency against poor policies, shocks, and structural changes faced real challenges in the first decade of the twenty-first century. This was underscored by the onset of the longest recession in the post–WWII era.

SELF EXAMINATION

True/False

1. From the beginning of industrial development in the United States, labor and management have enjoyed very cordial relations compared to those in other industrial nations.

2. Government has played an important role in the American economy and as an agent of economic development almost from the beginning of the establishment of the United States.

3. The Civil War had absolutely no positive impact on American economic development since it caused such widespread devastation to the economy and society.

4. "Progressivism" is a term used to describe the phenomenal period of American industrial growth between 1870 and 1900.

5. Up until 1920, most Americans lived outside of cities, in rural or small-town locations. Urbanization during and after the 1920s spurred the development of consumer goods industries.

6. The theoretical focus of the New Economics was on microeconomics, whereas before Keynes, the focus had been on macroeconomics.

7. Since the end of the 1950s, the role of multinational businesses has steadily increased as measured by these firms' output and sales.

8. The centerpiece efforts of Lyndon Johnson's Great Society programs were efforts aimed at reducing the

size of government in the economy and the dependence of American citizens on excessive amounts of government services.

9. Stagflation was a term adopted by economists in the 1970s to describe a national condition of lagging economic growth, high rates of unemployment, and high rates of inflation.

10. President Ronald Reagan defended his tax-cutting policies by citing the economic arguments advanced in the 1930s by J.M. Keynes.

11. The fiscal policies actually practiced during the Reagan years were similar to the anti-depressionary theories set forth by Keynes four decades earlier.

12. Although the federal deficit grew to incredible proportions during the Reagan years, America enjoyed a position of power in international affairs, enjoying a period of consistent trade surpluses.

13. An example of a structural shift in the American economy over the past forty years is the relative decline in manufacturing and the rise of service industries.

14. De-industrialization is a term used to describe the trend toward less government regulation in the economy.

15. The concept of "the public interest" presumes that certain governmental economic activities are essential to assure provision of goods and certain protections to the whole society that would not be provided by a pure market economy.

Multiple Choice

1. The New Economics is most closely associated with what period in American economic history?
   a. The rise of big business (1870–1900)
   b. The Progressive Era (1900–1920)
   c. The Great Depression (1932–1940)
   d. The Kennedy-Johnson Years (1960–1968)
   e. The Reagan Boom (1982–1988)

2. The economic policy practice by the British toward their American colonies was called:
   a. laissez-faire
   b. progressivism
   c. mercantilism
   d. economics of scale
   e. de-industrialization

3. Which of the following is an accurate commentary on America's economic growth record?
   a. Overall GDP/capita growth has been more than twice as great in the United States as in most of the industrial nations since 1870
   b. America's growth record was quite commendable up until the 1970s but since then has not been remarkable compared to the rest of the world

c. Only Japan has shown an impressive economic growth rate over the past thirty years
d. All of the above
e. None of the above

4. As an immediate cure to the depressed economic conditions of the 1930s, J.M. Keynes urged:
   a. an increase in government spending
   b. a return to higher rates of personal savings
   c. a reduction in business investments
   d. an increase in imports
   e. none of the above

5. Which of the following were important nineteenth-century pro-business activities undertaken by the federal government?
   a. Tariffs
   b. Subsidies and bounties for raw material development
   c. Enforcement of prohibitions on trade unions
   d. All of the above
   e. None of the above

6. Which of the following was probably *not* a cause of the stock market crash in 1929?
   a. Buying stocks on margin
   b. The sudden disappearance of buyers of stocks
   c. The belief that stocks were underpriced relative to their earnings
   d. The fact that Americans were saving too much

7. Which of the following initiatives was *not* part of the Great Society program?
   a. Civil rights legislation
   b. Deregulation of business
   c. Medicare and Medicaid
   d. Government aid to higher education
   e. Enlargement of social security benefits

8. The first American president to consciously follow the macroeconomic policy path suggested by Keynes was:
   a. Franklin Roosevelt
   b. Dwight Eisenhower
   c. John Kennedy
   d. Lyndon Johnson
   e. Ronald Reagan

9. The supply-side economics of the Reagan years emphasized:
   a. a tax cut to stimulate consumer spending
   b. a reduction of government regulation of business
   c. a purposeful increase in the federal deficit
   d. an increase in business taxes

10. The recession of 2007–2009 was notable because:
    a. it immediately followed a large bubble in housing prices
    b. it was the longest contraction since the Great Depression
    c. it pointed out fundamental weaknesses in the economy
    d. all of the above
    e. none of the above

ANSWERS TO SELF EXAMINATION

True/False

1. F
2. T
3. F
4. F
5. T
6. F
7. T
8. F
9. T
10. F
11. T
12. F
13. T
14. F
15. T

Mutiple Choice

1. D
2. C
3. B
4. A
5. D
6. C
7. B
8. C
9. B
10. D

Part II

Microeconomics

Chapter 5

When Firms Act as Price Makers: Competition Versus Monopoly

KEY TERMS

Firm

Industry

Pure competition

Monopolistic competition

Oligopoly

Monopoly

Explicit costs

Implicit costs

Accounting profits

Economic profits

Normal profit

Total fixed costs (TFC)

Total variable costs (TVC)

Short run

Long run

Average total costs (ATC)

Marginal cost (MC)

Total revenue (TR)

Productive efficiency

Allocative efficiency

Marginal revenue

MR = MC

Long-run competitive
  equilibrium

Economies of scale

Price fixing

Price discrimination

X-inefficiency

Natural monopoly

Industrial regulation

Fair return pricing

Cartel

Social regulation

CHAPTER SUMMARY

1. Industries and markets are comprised of individual firms. An industry does not necessarily equate to the market for a good. Economists define markets by criteria such as the substitutability of goods and geographic reach of the market.

2. Purely competitive markets are characterized by many independent sellers, homogeneous products, and no barriers to entry. These conditions place firms in the position of being price takers. Firms in a competitive market structure are compelled by the forces of competition to be efficient and, therefore, generate optimal results from a societal standpoint. In the long run, purely competitive firms are both allocatively efficient (P = MC) and productively efficient (P = minimum AC).

3. Economists posit three models of imperfect competition: monopolistic competition, oligopoly, and monopoly. In each of these, the seller can exercise some degree of control over price and quantity. Unlike the purely competitive market, imperfect competition tends to yield results in terms of prices and output that are not socially optimal. Generally, allocative efficiency is not achieved because P > MC, indicating underproduction of the product.

4. Monopoly market structures are fairly rare. When a monopoly exists, it is typically regulated as in the case of public utilities or natural monopolies. Regulatory commissions use fair-return pricing to control the exercise of monopoly pricing while permitting the regulated firm to cover costs and realize a fair return (normal profit) on investment.

5. The presence of large firms and potential market power does not necessarily mean that monopoly power can be exercised. Several factors can check market power, including public policy (antitrust) and potential competition.

6. Economic regulation emerged in the late 1800s principally in the form of industrial regulation of specific industries such as railroads, and subsequent forms of commercial transportation, and banking and financial services. Industrial regulation began to wane in the 1970s at the same time social regulation was on the rise.

7. Antitrust policy has been an enduring form of indirect regulation since 1890 with the passage of the Sherman Act outlawing restraint of trade that substantially lessens competition and efforts to create a monopoly.

SELF EXAMINATION

True/False

1. Generally a firm's price-making ability is inversely related to the number of similar sized firms operating in the market. For monopolistically competitive

firms, large advertising budgets are generally the rule.

2. From an accountant's view, profit is what is left over after all explicit costs of production and operations are paid.

3. One of the ways in which pure competition acts as a restraint on excessive profits and a stimulus for firms to be efficient is the ease of entry of other firms into the market.

4. In long-run equilibrium, firms operating in competitive markets will all earn economic profits.

5. Maximum efficiency for any firm exists at the level of output where P = MC.

6. The MC = MR rule of determining the socially optimal output level for a firm applies in the case of monopoly but not in the case of pure competition.

7. Fair-return pricing as applied to a public utility is undertaken to ensure that the utility earns a high and fair rate of economic profit.

8. The "contestable market" argument holds that inter-industry competition between giant firms in related, but not identical markets, tends to limit the price-making power of large firms.

9. For a monopoly firm, the firm's demand curve is downward-sloping to the right because its demand curve and the industry demand curve are identical.

10. The Sherman Anti-Trust Act of 1890 declared that "bigness" in business was illegal since it denied consumers the benefits of competition.

11. In recent decades, government policy has moved toward a looser and laxer enforcement of the letter of antitrust law.

12. "Deregulation" as an approach toward the various regulatory agencies was particularly popular in the 1980s and was in fact a central part of Ronald Reagan's supply-side strategy.

13. A firm's profits are maximized at the output level where average revenue equals average cost.

14. Economic theory maintains that firms in perfect competition exert considerable controls over prices.

15. A monopolist is a single seller of a unique product.

16. Economists view economic profit as the amount remaining after all implicit and explicit costs have been subtracted from total revenue.

17. If a firm sells more of its product in a perfectly competitive market, its total revenue must fall.

18. Economic profits tend to discourage firms from entering a market.

19. Antitrust laws are designed to prevent the formation of monopolies, curtail activities that restrain competition, and prohibit anti-competitive practices.

Multiple Choice

1. A firm in a market with many sellers, and relatively easy entry, and selling a product that is differenti-ated from similar products through advertising, is an example of:
   a. a purely competitive firm
   b. a monopolistic firm
   c. an oligopolistic firm
   d. a monopolistically competitive firm

2. An American wheat farmer operates in a market structure that is best described as:
   a. competitive
   b. monopolistic
   c. oligopolistic
   d. monopolistically competitive

3. In the short-run economic operation of a firm:
   a. total costs at first fall and then rise as production output is increased
   b. average total costs fall throughout the short-run period
   c. total fixed costs are unchanged
   d. all costs are variable costs

4. The marginal cost of any particular good is:
   a. under competition, always equal to its price
   b. the total cost of production divided by the number of goods produced
   c. under monopoly conditions, always greater than its price
   d. the additional cost of producing that particular good

Answer the next four questions using the following graph of a firm operating in competition:

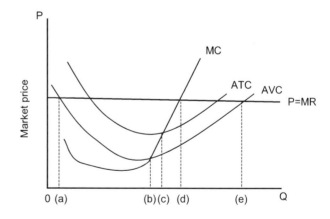

5. Average total costs are lowest at output level:
   a. (a)
   b. (b)
   c. (c)
   d. (d)
   e. (e)

6. Profit will be greatest at output level:
   a. (a)
   b. (b)
   c. (c)
   d. (d)
   e. (e)

7. Productive efficiency is obtained at output level:
   a. (a)
   b. (b)
   c. (c)
   d. (d)
   e. (e)

8. Beyond output the firm would break even, earning no profit in the short run at output level:
   a. (a)
   b. (b)
   c. (c)
   d. (d)
   e. (e)
   f. none of the above

9. In setting a price for a public utility according to the doctrine of fair-return pricing, regulatory authorities should set the price and output:
   a. where MC = MR
   b. where MC is lowest
   c. where MC = ATC
   d. where ATC = P
   e. where ATC is lowest

10. A public utility regulated by an independent regulatory commission according to the policy of "fair-return pricing":
    a. has little individual incentive to act to lower unit costs
    b. must provide service to all who are willing to purchase its service at the regulated price
    c. is assured, legally, of never going bankrupt
    d. all of the above
    e. none of the above

11. Which of the following was the first federal independent regulatory commission?
    a. The Federal Power Commission
    b. The Atomic Energy Commission
    c. The Securities and Exchange Commission
    d. The Interstate Commerce Commission
    e. The Federal Reserve System

12. The immediate effect of deregulation in the airlines industry was:
    a. an increase in air fares
    b. an increase in the number of new airports
    c. an increase in government efforts to set air fares and assign air routes
    d. a decline in air passengers
    e. an increase in the number of airlines

13. An example of social regulation is:
    a. the Environmental Protection Agency
    b. the Interstate Commerce Commission
    c. industrial policy
    d. the Sherman Anti-Trust Act
    e. all of the above

14. Which of the following statements is correct?
    a. A normal profit occurs when total revenue minus total costs equals zero.
    b. Total costs equal the sum of fixed costs and marginal costs.
    c. Total fixed costs reside below total variable costs.
    d. An economic profit occurs when total revenue minus explicit costs is greater than zero.

15. A perfectly competitive firm will face a demand curve that is:
    a. vertical and anchored at the market quantity
    b. horizontal and coinciding with the market price
    c. downward-sloping within a narrow range of prices
    d. shifting rightward
    e. a parabola

16. The ideal purpose of antitrust laws is to:
    a. maintain competitors
    b. maintain a monopoly
    c. maintain the status quo
    d. maintain competition
    e. make lawyers and expert witnesses wealthy

17. Government regulation of business is economically justified when:
    a. the government prefers intervention to laissez-faire
    b. property rights are poorly defined, economies of scale exist, or there is imperfect information
    c. people have an anti-capitalist attitude
    d. profits are being earned

ANSWERS TO SELF EXAMINATION

True/False

1. T	11. F
2. T	12. T
3. T	13. T
4. F	14. F
5. F	15. F
6. T	16. T
7. F	17. F
8. F	18. F
9. F	19. F
10. T	

Multiple Choice

1. D
2. A
3. C
4. D
5. B
6. D
7. C
8. F

9. D
10. D
11. D
12. E
13. A
14. A
15. B
16. D
17. B

Chapter 6

The Economics of Externalities and the Environment

KEY TERMS

Pollution
Exclusion
Rival consumption
Free rider problem
Externalities
Coase Theorem

Emission charge
Command-and-
  control regulation
Emission standard
Marketable pollution
  rights

CHAPTER SUMMARY

1. Environmental problems concern pollution, wildlife and habitat preservation, nonrenewable resource management, and environmental equity. Pollution occurs when emissions of natural and manmade wastes and byproducts degrade the services of the natural environment. Wildlife and habitat are renewable resources that are critical to the services of the environment. The environment is a closed system with the capacity to recycle and dilute wastes and byproducts. Nonrenewable natural resources are deposits of mineral resources. When that capacity is exceeded, environmental degradation occurs.

2. The services of the environment are collectively consumed. In the absence of property rights or governmental intervention, all are free to use and abuse the services of the environment. The collective consumption of environmental services gives rise to externalities. When sizable externalities are present, the market will not be capable of bringing about an efficient allocation.

3. External benefits arise when the production or consumption of a product confers benefits upon third parties. Building park-like playgrounds may yield external environmental and community benefits, but there is little incentive for the private sector to produce these benefits in adequate amounts. A subsidy might encourage private sector activities that improve the environment.

4. External costs are experienced by third parties when the production cost or consumption of a product results in pollution or some other kind of environmental degradation. The market overproduces the product because it fails to count the social cost of pollution. Regulatory standards or a tax on polluters can remedy the problem.

5. Social choices about the pursuit of environmental improvement are subject to the opportunity cost principle. For example, pollution abatement entails a sacrifice of alternative goods and services.

6. Determining the optimal effort for alleviating environmental damage can be accomplished with benefit-cost analysis. Ideally, environmental improvement should be undertaken to the extent where the last increment produced adds as much to total social benefit as it adds to total social cost—that is, marginal social benefit equals marginal social cost.

7. The Coase Theorem argues that conferring either a right to pollute or a right to a pollution-free environment can lead to an efficient solution for offsetting the social cost if transaction costs are zero. This suggests that property rights can provide a basis for negotiating the correction of external costs. However, society's approach to the matter must consider the magnitude of transaction costs and the costs of adjudication that may be associated with the administration and enforcement of property rights.

8. An emission charge or tax conveys the proper economic incentives to regulate pollution. When the charge is greater than a firm's marginal cost of cleaning the pollution, the company will choose to internalize the cost of pollution. When the marginal cost of cleaning exceeds the emission charge, the firm will pay the charge rather than clean the pollution.

9. Command-and-control regulation relies on enforce-

ment of emissions standards and the requirement of specific emission-control devices for selected sources of pollution. This type of environmental management is rather inflexible and does not necessarily create economic incentives to control pollution. However, the EPA had favored its use because it was regarded as less costly and more technically feasible than emissions charges. In the years since the passage of the 1990 amendments to the Clean Air Act, emissions regulation has become more market-based with the introduction of tradable emissions allowances for sulfur dioxide.

10. Subsidies encourage environmental improvement. Federal subsidies to state and local governments for waste treatment plants are a dominant expenditure.

11. Markets for pollution rights are gradually evolving. Marketable emissions allowances have demonstrated promise for efficiently achieving air quality standards. Firms with high cleaning costs will want to buy allowances that permit them to pollute more, while firms with low cleaning costs will sell allowances and pollute commensurately less.

12. Recent legislative attention has focused on air pollution problems. New standards and policies have been developed to address acid rain, toxic emissions, stratospheric ozone depletion, and global warming.

13. Land use carries its own environmental problems, notably soil erosion and landfills. Soil erosion is costly, but difficult to prevent because of problems in policy coordination. Landfills are a consequence of trash creation. Much solid waste disposal could be curtailed through recycling and user fees.

14. Equity issues with respect to the environment include the distribution of the burden of social costs, the benefit distribution of corrective policies, and the burden of corrective measures across the distribution of income. Although environmental degradation is a universal social problem, low-income citizens appear to experience most of the cost burdens. Corrective measures will alter the composition of output to the disadvantage of some sectors of the economy, but to the advantage of others.

15. Finally, environmental problems raise the issue of intergenerational equity. What kind of environment do we owe to future generations? Society has to take the long view about environmental policy if it is to incorporate intergenerational equity into its choices in the present.

SELF EXAMINATION

True/False

1. The services of the environment can be classified as common property.
2. Economists generally favor elimination of all pollution as an environmental policy.
3. A pollution tax can cause the internalization of the external cost of pollution.
4. If a firm had to purchase "rights" or permits to pollute, external costs might be more efficiently reduced than by command-and-control regulation.
5. Emission fees dissuade firms from polluting by appealing to morality and business ethics.
6. The best way to encourage recycling is to force people to do it.
7. A community should pursue policies that reduce the waste stream to zero.
8. Pollution can include sources other than manmade wastes.
9. Collective consumption of environmental services makes environmental problems easily subject to market solutions.
10. Improving environmental quality entails the sacrifice of alternative goods and activities.
11. Efforts to improve environmental quality have diminished in the last five to ten years.
12. The 1990 Clean Air Act adopts no new measures for environmental improvement.
13. Stratospheric ozone depletion is a small policy concern.
14. Endangered species are part of the environmental problem.
15. The qualities of exclusivity and rival consumption apply to the use of the atmosphere.

Multiple Choice

1. Firms with high cleaning costs will react to a low emission fee by:
   a. cleaning their emissions
   b. paying the fee
   c. neither cleaning emissions nor paying the fee
   d. relocating to countries with high emissions fees

2. The environment can be classified as a:
   a. private good
   b. public good
   c. negative externality
   d. vice good

3. The purpose of offering subsidies to polluters is to:
   a. reduce the polluters' costs of cleaning up pollution
   b. increase the polluters' cost of cleaning up pollution
   c. provide an incentive to pollute more
   d. redistribute income to polluting firms

4. Exhaustible resources such as fossil fuels can be managed by market allocation because:
   a. common property rights and the qualities of public goods prevail
   b. the government should not intervene
   c. oil suppliers need high incomes
   d. private property and the qualities of private goods apply

5. If a system is "closed," it means that:
   a. wastes must be recycled in the long run or environmental quality will degrade
   b. wastes are injected from outside and degrade environmental quality
   c. patterns are fixed
   d. free-riding must develop

6. Your neighbor plays her stereo so loud that you cannot study or sleep. You are experiencing:
   a. mind control
   b. a positive externality
   c. a negative externality
   d. the better half of college life
   e. accounting costs

7. An internal cost refers to:
   a. direct production costs borne by the producers
   b. costs spilled over to third parties
   c. deeply felt costs
   d. yield from the sale of a product

8. The equality between the marginal social benefits and marginal social costs of pollution abatement ensures:
   a. negative net social benefits
   b. maximum net social benefits
   c. the proper income distribution
   d. minimum net social benefits

9. The theorem described by Ronald Coase suggests that:
   a. the existence of property rights can result in inefficient solutions to externalities if transactions and enforcement costs are negligible
   b. the existence of property rights cannot result in efficient solutions to externalities unless transactions and enforcement costs are substantial
   c. only goodwill can successfully offset externalities
   d. economists have no useful propositions about compensating for externalities

10. One economically efficient means of financing solid waste disposal into landfills is to:
    a. pass through the costs in general taxes
    b. delay landfill sitings for years
    c. set quotas on the amount of garbage a household or business can generate
    d. impose user fees or tipping fees

11. The equity issue regarding environmental quality involves:
    a. whether fees or regulations are used
    b. whether optimal levels of environmental management are achieved
    c. whether there is fair cost and benefit sharing for environmental improvements
    d. making sure that people get equal benefits from EPA expenditures on the environment

12. The Kyoto Protocol:
    a. imposed more stringent emission reductions on developing nations
    b. met targets for emissions reductions
    c. exempted the United States because it had a head start on environmental improvement
    d. has been superseded by the Copenhagen Accord's goal to hold the global temperature increase to two degrees Celsius

Problems and Thought Questions

1. The emissions of waste chemicals and schedule for cleaning costs for a plastics manufacturer are found below:

Chemical Emissions per Day (pounds)	Marginal Cost of Cleaning
3,000	$7
6,000	8
9,000	9
12,000	10

   a. If the EPA sets an emission fee of $9 and the plant's discharge is 3,000 pounds, what is the best economic decision for the firm? Why?
   b. With a $9 emission fee, what is the firm's best choice if its emissions are 12,000 pounds per day?

2. Suppose a smoke-emitting factory covers a nearby florist's greenhouse with soot, blocking out sunlight and killing $6,000 worth of plants per year. Washing the glass each day would cost $9,500 per year to remedy the problem. Alternatively, a smokestack filter would cost $3,000 and last about nine years.
   a. What is the efficient solution to the problem?
   b. What should the factory do if the greenhouse is granted a legal right to soot-free windows? Explain.
   c. What should the florist do if the factory is granted the right to emit smoke and soot?

3. Compare the advantages and disadvantages of tradable emissions allowances versus command-and-control regulation.

4. Label the following diagram in such a way as to show the community's optimal level of pollution abatement.

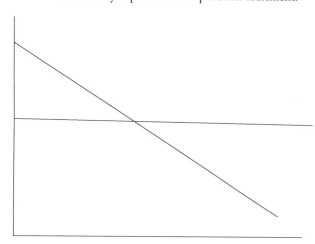

ANSWERS TO SELF EXAMINATION

True/False

1. T
2. F
3. T
4. T
5. F
6. F
7. F
8. T
9. F
10. T
11. F
12. F
13. F
14. T
15. F

Multiple Choice

1. B
2. B
3. A
4. D
5. A
6. C
7. A
8. B
9. A
10. D
11. C
12. D

Problems and Thought Questions

1.
    a. clean the discharge (MCC < fee)
    b. pay the fee (MCC > fee)

2.
    a. buy the filter
    b. buy the filter
    c. buy the filter

4.

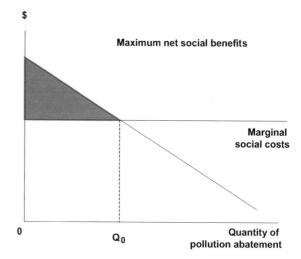

Chapter 7

Health-Care Issues

KEY TERMS

Moral hazard   Third-party payers

First-dollar coverage   Supplier-induced demand

National health insurance

CHAPTER SUMMARY

1. The health-care sector's rapidly rising costs and expenditures, explosion of new technology, and swiftly evolving industry structure have drawn considerable attention. As health-care expenditures claim a greater percentage of GDP, and as medical services prices increase at a more rapid rate than the prices for all goods and services, there emerges a public perception of a problem. The problem is compounded by varying viewpoints about whether or not health care is a public good and a basic right. Some forms of health care possess, at least partially, the characteristics of public or social goods; others are clearly private goods. Health-care services are often perceived as merit goods to be relegated to provision through government.

2. Like other goods, increased provision of health-care services is subject to the opportunity cost of sacrificing other goods. Economic reality is that health care cannot be free.

3. The receipt of health-care services has to be distinguished from health financing.

4. The demand for physicians' and hospital services is very price inelastic. Third-party payers dominate the financing of health care. The presence of third-party payers and health-care suppliers' ability to dictate consumption introduce a unique form of moral hazard wherein health-care consumers and medical practitioners do not have a strong incentive to contain costs. The demand side of the market includes an estimated 19 to 45 million uninsured people.

5. The supply side of the market includes four categories: independent physicians' services, hospital care, health maintenance organizations, and other health-care facilities. Technological and institutional changes have admitted a greater degree of competition among providers.

6. Third-party payers account for well over 80 percent of health-care spending. Total health expenditures have reached $2 trillion. Among fastest rates of spending growth are prescription drugs and administration. Sixty percent of health expenditures are for physicians' services, hospital care, and nursing home care.

7. Aggregate health expenditures and health expenditures per capita are forecast to double by 2015. Health expenditures claim about 16 percent of GDP and are projected to continue rising. Medical services prices are also rising more rapidly than the general level of prices.

8. The number of people without health insurance in the United States could be as large as 45 million. Nonetheless, private insurance and public sources of health-care financing have increased the percentage of the population covered from 10 percent in 1940 to at least 84 percent by 2004. Out-of-pocket spending for personal health care has trended downward to about 15 percent. The U.S. system of employer-based health insurance emerged during World War II and was encouraged by public policy.

9. The rise in health spending is an international trend, but the United States has tended to exhibit faster growth. Health-care services generally cost more in the United States compared to other OECD countries. This has fueled higher spending per capita. Several sources are identifiable as contributing to higher expenditure in the United States including: rising living standards, an aging population, third-party payers, technological progress, effects of

medical malpractice, market power, administrative complexity, and high prices.

10. Society must choose between market versus non-market mechanisms for allocating health care. Society's policy choices are generally a matter of establishing what combination of market and nonmarket allocation mechanisms should be used to provide high quality health care on a wide basis while restricting costs. Cost containment has seized much of the attention with prospective payment systems and prepaid health care. These innovations have combined with the launch of new competition in the industry.

11. Health-care allocation and financing will remain high-priority issues because of an aging population. Management of the allocation mechanism to maximize access to high quality health care at affordable prices poses perhaps one of the most difficult challenges for the U.S. economy. Proposals for health-care reform range from a government-directed national system to tax-favored and more market-based approaches. The Patient Protection and Affordable Care Act marks a significant increase in government's role, but in a hybrid fashion, of which the ultimate course and results are yet to be known.

SELF EXAMINATION

True/False

1. Vaccinations produce a spillover benefit.
2. The "play or pay" approach to health-care reform gives people tax credits for purchasing health-care insurance.
3. More health-care services can be provided to cover the uninsured without a sacrifice of alternative goods.
4. The American Medical Association has historically strongly favored increases in the number and type of health-care providers.
5. Moral hazard arises when insurance causes people to misrepresent risk and be less careful about minimizing costs.
6. Outpatient services have been the area of most active competition in recent years in the health-care industry.
7. Antitrust cases have concluded that physicians acting in concert do not possess market power.
8. Countries with "socialized medicine" are able to provide health care for free.
9. The American Medical Association has acted to restrict the supply of medical practitioners.
10. HMOs are prepaid health-care plans.
11. The Patient Protection and Affordable Care Act nationalizes the health insurance industry.

12. The Patient Protection and Affordable Care Act requires some uninsured people to obtain insurance through state-organized "exchanges" or else pay a penalty.

Multiple Choice

1. The concept of "managed care" refers to:
   a. reliance upon a national health-insurance plan
   b. diagnoses related groups
   c. fee for service
   d. reliance upon preventive medicine and prepaid health care to contain costs
   e. reliance upon market supply and demand to resolve the health-care crisis

2. Which of the following categories absorbs the largest percentage of health-care expenditures in the United States?
   a. Hospital care
   b. Nursing-home care
   c. Physicians' services
   d. Home health care

3. The inelastic demand for health-care services indicates that:
   a. consumers greatly reduce their purchases of health-care services when prices rise
   b. consumers have little alternative but to pay the higher prices when health-care prices rise
   c. total expenditures for health care will rise when prices fall
   d. total expenditures for health-care services will remain constant despite price changes

4. If people could sell transplantable human organs:
   a. a greater quantity would be supplied
   b. less transplant surgery would be conducted
   c. people will have a strong incentive to murder their relatives and sell the decedent's organs
   d. organ transplants will be cheaper

5. Some analysts argue that the rising percentage of GDP going to health care:
   a. reveals society's desire to allocate fewer resources to health care
   b. reveals society's desire to allocate more resources to health care
   c. cannot be explained
   d. is a statistical illusion

Answer the next five questions using the following alternatives:

   a Government-financed national health insurance
   b. Personal income-tax credits for buyers of health insurance

c. Employer-provided health insurance with government backup insurance

d. Expanded Medicare and Medicaid

6. Which of the above alternatives is known as the "play or pay" approach to health-care reform?

7. The outlays for health care will likely be greatest under which of the alternatives?

8. Which alternative places the largest financial burden upon employers?

9. Which alternative is likely to provide the most comprehensive coverage?

10. Which alternative will allow individuals the greatest choice in selecting among various insurance alternatives?

11. The health-care reform approach that provides tax relief if people buy health insurance is:
   a. the "play or pay" proposal
   b. national health insurance
   c. the tax credit proposal
   d. tax-based incomes policy
   e. Medicare

12. Medical malpractice suits:
   a. have resulted in increased malpractice insurance premiums and added several dollars to the cost of a hospital stay or doctor's office visit
   b. have resulted in decreased malpractice insurance premiums and subtracted several dollars from the cost of a hospital stay or doctor's office visit
   c. have had no effect on malpractice insurance premiums
   d. actively discourage wasteful defensive medicine

Problems and Thought Questions

1. Use a production-possibilities curve to illustrate why health care cannot be a free good. Explain.

2. Show how the use of third-party payers has influenced the health-care market.

3. List and explain the various explanations for the rapid rise in health-care costs.

4. What are the major health care reform proposals? Explain how well each might work to:
   a. increase access to health care
   b. constrain rising costs
   c. maintain the quality of care
   d. maintain individual choice

ANSWERS TO SELF EXAMINATION

True/False

1. T
2. F
3. F
4. F
5. T
6. T
7. F
8. F
9. T
10. T
11. F
12. T

Multiple Choice

1. D
2. A
3. B
4. A
5. B
6. C
7. A
8. C
9. A
10. B
11. C
12. A

Problems and Thought Questions

1.

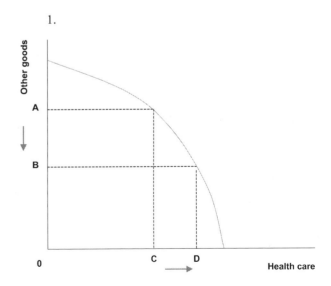

To gain CD health care requires a sacrifice (cost) of AB other goods.

2.

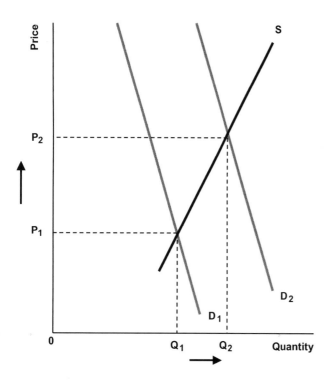

Chapter 8

Factor Markets:
Pricing and Productivity

KEY TERMS

Reservation wage

Marginal resource cost

Derived demand

Marginal product

Law of diminishing returns

Marginal revenue product

Least-cost rule

Interest rate

Economic rent

Monopsony

Exclusive (craft) unionism

Inclusive (industrial)
    unionism

Bilateral monopoly

CHAPTER SUMMARY

1. Factor markets determine the payments in the form of wages, interest, and rent paid to those resources used in the production of final goods. Factor markets are driven by essentially the same rules that operate in finished goods markets. The supply of a productive resource—labor, capital, or land—is principally determined by scarcity and opportunity cost. The demand for a particular factor depends on the demand for the product that resource is used to produce (a derived demand) and the productivity of the particular resource. In ordinary resource markets, equilibrium exists at the price and quantity combination where MRP = MRC. That is to say, a particular resource will be hired up to the point where the added cost of hiring the last unit is just covered by the additional revenue generated by that unit of the resource.

2. Firms, of course, may choose among different resources in the production of goods. They may hire labor or they may use machines to do the same tasks. An optimal combination of resource use is obtained when, in the mix of resource use, the enterprise allocates its spending so that the marginal output of each dollar spent on any factor hired is the same as the marginal output per dollar of any other factor. This least-cost rule is stated algebraically as:

$$\frac{MP_L}{P_L} = \frac{MP_C}{P_C}$$

The profit-maximizing combination of labor and capital when each are hired in competitive resource markets is:

$$\frac{MRP_L}{P_L} = \frac{MRP_C}{P_C} = 1$$

3. Interest payments are associated with the use of capital. Interest rates are associated with the rates of return on investment projects. The interest rate is the "price" of borrowing for investment purposes and "price" received by individuals who are willing to lend funds for investment purposes.

4. Rent is associated with fixed resources, typically land (or capital). Rent is viewed as an unproductive payment because rent does not have the typical incentive function associated with it; fluctuations in rental payments will produce no variation in the amount of the resource supplied.

5. Monopsony is defined as a single buyer. When monopsony exists in the resource market, the employer of the resource exercises market power to underprice the resource and employ less than the allocatively efficient amount compared to equivalently competitive circumstances.

6. Unions can attempt to raise the price of labor through several approaches: encouraging greater demand for labor, restricting the supply of labor in the case of an exclusive or craft union, and demanding a union minimum (reservation) wage in the case of an inclusive or industrial union. Bilateral monopoly is a special case of a monopsony employer confronted with an industrial union acting as a monopoly seller of labor.

7. The impact of the internationalization of labor markets upon wages and employment has gathered attention in recent years. No lasting adverse affects are evident.

SELF EXAMINATION

True/False

1. Productive factors are always in competition with one another since productive factors are by their nature interchangeable.
2. By derived demand we refer to the fact that the demand for final goods is really determined by the costs (paid to productive factors) of resources used in producing that good.
3. From the firm's point of view, its MRP cure and its MRC curve for a particular productive resource are, respectively, its demand and supply curves for that resource.
4. The least-cost rule maintains that employers should always try to keep wages low even if the result is a decline in output.
5. The biggest determinant of labor productivity is the quantity and quality of tools and capital a worker has to work with.
6. If the productivity of a resource rises, we would expect a firm, *ceteris paribus*, to buy less of it.
7. Rent is the payment made to the resource of labor.
8. Capital markets are subject to essentially the same factor-market rules that apply in labor markets.
9. The law of diminishing returns states that additional units of labor added to a fixed amount of capital will result in incrementally smaller additions to output.
10. Marginal revenue product is the additional revenue realized from the change in output attributable to hiring an additional unit of labor.
11. The demand for labor will be more inelastic if other resources can be readily substituted for labor.
12. Forced labor is associated with coercive labor markets.

Multiple Choice

1. The marginal revenue product of a factor input:
   a. depends on the productivity of the factor and the price of the good produced by that factor
   b. always equals MRC
   c. is the same as the supply curve for that factor
   d. rises with the hiring of additional factors

2. The demand for a particular productive factor is to some extent determined by:
   a. the price of other factors
   b. the availability of substitutes for that factor
   c. the price of final goods that factor will be hired to produce
   d. all of the above
   e. none of the above

3. Derived demand is best illustrated by which of the following cases?
   a. The demand for capital rises as a result of a rise in wages
   b. MRC is greater than MRP
   c. Due to an improving economy, sales of autos rise and GM hires more workers
   d. American rates of productivity increase

4. Due to rising interest rates, GM decides to slow down the introduction of new robots on its assembly line and cancels an earlier plan to reduce its production work force. This is an example of:
   a. the effect of changes in productivity
   b. derived demand
   c. the factor interchangeability
   d. the law of increasing cost

5. A firm seeking to maximize efficiency and profits:
   a. should spend as little on productive factors as possible
   b. should hire factors up to that point where each dollar of input for each productive factor is equal in output value to one dollar
   c. should hire resources up to the point where all resources have identical marginal products
   d. all of the above
   e. none of the above

6. If wage rates fall, *ceteris paribus*:
   a. labor may be substituted for machines in the production process
   b. the MRC of labor will rise
   c. MRP will rise
   d. all of the above
   e. none of the above

7. If interest rates fall, *ceteris paribus*:
   a. savers may save less
   b. the MRC of capital will also fall
   c. capital is more attractive to a firm hiring it as a factor of production
   d. all of the above
   e. none of the above

8. Which of the following facts may contribute to the rising price of real estate in downtown Seattle?
   a. An increase in demand for downtown Seattle office space
   b. There is an absolute limit to the possible geographic size of downtown Seattle
   c. The supply of land in downtown Seattle is inelastic
   d. All of the above
   e. None of the above

9. Which of the following generalizations is true?
   a. If the resource cost to total cost ratio is low, resource demand will be elastic
   b. If product demand is elastic, resource demand will tend to be elastic
   c. Resource demand will probably be more elastic in the short run versus the long run
   d. Only labor demand can be inelastic

10. An effort to raise members' wages by limiting the supply of qualified workers is an example of:
    a. exclusive unionism
    b. inclusive unionism
    c. "broad-based organizing"
    d. all of the above
    e. none of the above

11. Bilateral monopoly:
    a. means that monopoly power resides exclusively with the labor-side of the market
    b. holds the possibility that market power on the part of both the sole employer and an industrial union might be neutralized
    c. is a geometric shape that isolates the gains from exploiting labor
    d. is always preferable to competition

12. Studies show that:
    a. immigrants ruin U.S. labor markets
    b. workers prefer the simplicity of coercive labor markets
    c. a 10 percent increase in immigration produces a 10 percent decrease in wages
    d. immigration has exerted a small impact upon wages

ANSWERS TO SELF EXAMINATION

True/False

1. F
2. F
3. T
4. F
5. T
6. F
7. F
8. T
9. T
10. T
11. F
12. T

Multiple Choice

1. A
2. D
3. C
4. C
5. B
6. A
7. D
8. D
9. B
10. A
11. B
12. D

Chapter 9

The Distribution of Income: Dividing the Economic Pie

KEY TERMS

Functional distribution of income
Distribution of personal income

Lorenz curve
Gini ratio

CHAPTER SUMMARY

1. The functional distribution of income relates to the shares of income earned by the factors of production in the form of wages, rents, interest, and profits. Labor's share is the largest proportion, and a relatively stable percentage, of national income. The distribution of personal income is concerned with how personal income received is distributed among individuals, families, and households. The personal income distribution varies by factors such ethnicity, gender, education, occupation, marital status, age, and other factors.

2. The Lorenz curve is an analytical device for visualizing the degree of income inequality. The Gini ratio or Gini coefficient is a summary statistic about income inequality that can be related to the Lorenz curve. A Gini coefficient of 0 means that income is equally distributed. A value of 100 is interpreted as total inequality. The Gini coefficient has been gradually rising since the 1970s, although there is some equivocation about the true increase in income inequality in the United States.

3. Factors influencing the distribution of income and its trend include: ability, education and training, wealth, discrimination, random events, intellectual property, labor unions, and immigration.

4. A tradeoff exists between income equality and economic efficiency. Vigorous efforts to redistribute could diminish incentives to work, save, and invest, thereby hampering economic performance. The bureaucracy required to operate a tax and transfer payment system diverts resources away from productive activities in the private sector, which is also detrimental to economic output. Nevertheless, society will likely have to engage in redistributive efforts to some degree in order to offset or avert certain social problems.

5. The distribution of income in the world is highly unequal and inequality appears to be increasing. Growing inequality is attributable mainly to income differences between countries rather than significant changes within countries.

6. Rising income inequality in the United States does not appear to have caused increased inequality in happiness.

SELF EXAMINATION

True/False

1. White Americans receive average incomes twice as high, on average, as black Americans.
2. Statistically speaking, the best odds for having a high level of discretionary income are to be a white male, college-educated, and employed as a manager.

Indicate whether questions 3 through 7 are true or false based upon the following diagram.

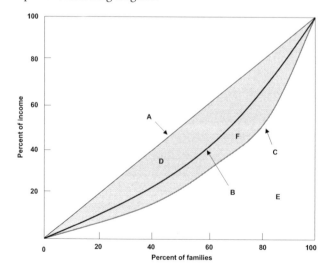

3. The diagram above is best used to illustrate the functional distribution of income.

4. The diagram above shows possible locations for the Lorenz curve.

5. Line A is the line of perfect inequality.

6. The movement from curve C to curve B represents a move toward greater income equality.

7. Areas D + F divided by the sum of areas D + F + E is a means for estimating the Gini ratio.

8. The marginal productivity theory suggests that differences in income and wealth are due to differences in productive effort.

9. In the United States there has been little change in the distribution of personal income since 1944.

10. On average, Asians earn more than whites, followed by Hispanics, followed by blacks, in descending order.

11. Based on the few good studies of the distribution of income from an international perspective, one can conclude that income is rather evenly distributed among nations.

12. Evidence demonstrates that happiness rises at a geometric rate relative to increases in personal income.

Multiple Choice

1. Which of the following generalizations is true?
   a. After counting taxes and transfers, there is a very dramatic equalization of income in the United States.
   b. The lowest quintile of income recipients accounts for less than 5 percent of family income.
   c. After taxes and subsidies are factored in, the lowest two quintiles of American wage earners receive the same share of income as they did before.
   d. Only the top income quintile gains after tax and transfer redistributions.

2. The Lorenz curve is an analytic tool principally used for:
   a. comparing types of employment and levels of income
   b. examining government transfer payments
   c. comparing world income levels
   d. examining the distribution of income

3. The efficiency versus equity tradeoff refers to:
   a. buying common stocks versus savings in a commercial bank account
   b. greater efficiency making people less generous in charitable giving
   c. a fairer distribution of income arising only from gains in economic efficiency
   d. the pursuit of greater income equality requiring a sacrifice in economic efficiency

Answer questions 4 and 5 based upon the following diagram.

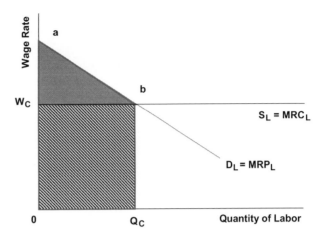

4. The share of income received by labor is:
   a. $W_C ab$
   b. $0abQ_C$
   c. $0W_C bQ_C$
   d. none of above

5. The share of income going to capital is:
   a. $W_C ab$
   b. $0abQ_C$
   c. $0W_C bQ_C$
   d. none of above

6. The shares of national income from largest to smallest are:
   a. compensation of employees, corporate profits, proprietors' income, interest, and rent
   b. rent, interest, proprietors' income, corporate profits, and compensation of employees
   c. proprietors' income, rent, compensation of employees, and corporate profits
   d. corporate profits, proprietors' income, rent, and compensation of employees

7. Comparative Gini ratios reveal:
   a. the United States to have the greatest income inequality among OECD nations
   b. the United States to have the least income inequality among OECD nations
   c. the United States is above the average Gini ratio for OECD nations
   d. the United States is below the average Gini ratio for OECD nations

8. Labor's share of national income:
   a. has been about 65 percent over the long run
   b. has been a 33 percent over the long run
   c. is dominated by corporate profits
   d. is actually derived from rental income

9. The distribution of personal income:
   a. is explained by the lack of fairness in the economic system
   b. can be explained by examining differences in ability, education, training, experience, ownership of property, and effort
   c. defies rational explanation
   d. has led to a very high level of dissatisfaction in the United States compared to other advanced countries with less income inequality
   e. has been the direct cause of nearly every rebellion in the United States beginning with the Whiskey Rebellion in the early 1790s

10. Straightforward generalizations about the distribution of income are:
   a. complicated by the choice of economic units, income measure chosen, and the quality of the data available
   b. indicate that things are really unfair
   c. concrete and readily supported by available data
   d. none of the above

ANSWERS TO SELF EXAMINATION

True/False

1. F
2. F
3. F
4. T
5. F
6. F
7. T
8. T
9. F
10. T
11. F
12. F

Multiple Choice

1. B
2. D
3. D
4. C
5. A
6. A
7. C
8. A
9. B
10. A

Chapter 10

Government Expenditures and Taxation

KEY TERMS

Fiscal federalism
Government purchases
Government transfer
  payments
Ability-to-pay principle
Benefits-received principle
Average tax rate
Marginal tax rate
Proportional tax
Progressive tax

Regressive tax
Statutory incidence
Economic incidence
Excess burden or
  deadweight loss
Value-added tax
Progressive consumption tax
Integration of corporate and
  personal income taxes

CHAPTER SUMMARY

1. Public sector intervention in the economy is justified on four general grounds: market imperfections, market failures, instabilities, and ethical and political dilemmas.

2. Government expenditures as a share of GDP have risen from 7 percent in 1902 to more than 37 percent by 2006. The growth of the federal government is traced in part to the enactment of the Sixteenth Amendment, which gave the federal government a virtually limitless power to tax. Wars, arms races, and greater commitment to social programs helped push spending higher over the past century. The emergence of fiscal federalism as an approach to government finance placed the federal government in the position of using its considerable capacity to raise revenue and redistribute it among state and local governments.

3. Government spending takes two forms: purchases or transfer payments. The distinction is important because purchases directly use resources and are counted in GDP, whereas transfer payments change the distribution of claims upon resources.

4. The design of a tax system may be guided by either the ability-to-pay or the benefits-received principle. Taxes are also judged by the rate of taxation as a proportion of taxpayers' income: proportional, progressive, or regressive. The various taxes imposed can be evaluated based upon these criteria.

5. Tax incidence is divided into two categories: statutory incidence and economic incidence. The statutory incidence refers to who has the legal obligation to pay the tax. The economic incidence of a tax considers who actually bears the burden of the tax after the effects of burden shifting are considered.

6. Taxes typically impose losses in economic efficiency. Better quality taxes raise revenue while generating small excess burdens from lost efficiency.

7. Alternative tax polices seek to generate additional revenue and partly or fully replace income taxes in order to avoid the efficiency distortions of the income tax. Most alternatives involve transitioning to consumption-based taxes.

8. Corporate taxes place a significant burden upon capital income by imposing high marginal tax rates that are compounded by the effect of double taxation on the portion of corporate profits distributed as dividends.

9. Personal income and payroll tax burdens in the United States are moderate when compared to those in other countries. U.S. tax rates on corporate income are among the highest for developed countries.

10. The majority of government spending is devoted to transfer payments. Projected expenditures for Social Security are regarded as precursors of an approaching entitlement crisis. Income maintenance expenditures to offset poverty consume sizable shares of government budgets, but do alleviate the severity of poverty.

SELF EXAMINATION

True/False

1. The highest rate bracket in the current federal personal income tax is 90 percent.
2. The increased role of the central government was enabled by the Sixteenth Amendment to the U.S. Constitution.
3. Government purchases do not contribute to national product.
4. A government transfer payment does not directly contribute to national output.
5. The concept of "diminishing marginal utility for money income" is an argument that could be used to justify higher tax rate taxes on higher income individuals.
6. The federal government is required by law to balance its budget annually, but state and local governments are not required to attain budget balance.
7. The primary tax source for the federal government is the personal income tax.
8. A progressive tax is one in which average effective tax rates decline as income rises.
9. A regressive tax will fall most heavily upon those least able to pay the tax.
10. The property tax is the most proportional of all taxes.
11. Tax incidence refers to who actually pays a tax, often persons different from those upon whom the tax is initially levied.
12. Poverty rates in the United States have been steadily rising since 1960.
13. The fact that all Americans pay 6.2 percent on the first $106,800 (in 2011) of earned income in social security taxes means that the social security payroll tax is proportional.
14. Since corporations "don't vote," they are a politically attractive target for taxation, but since taxes on corporations very often are passed on, the taxes levied may be actually regressive in effect.
15. One proposal to raise more revenue for the federal government is to impose a national consumption tax.

Multiple Choice

1. The filings of corporate tax returns reveal that most corporations:
   a. paid no corporation income taxes
   b. are in the 34, 35, or 38 percent marginal tax bracket
   c. paid a 65 percent corporate tax
   d. are seeking bankruptcy protection to avoid paying taxes

2. Examining government budget trends since the 1960s, it is apparent that:
   a. government outlays as a share of GDP have steadily risen
   b. dollar outlays by all governments have risen but expenditures as a share of GDP have fallen
   c. the increase in total tax burden is mostly the result of state and local tax changes
   d. no governmental unit makes serious efforts to balance its budget

3. Which of the following is the largest outlay in the Federal budget?
   a. Income security
   b. National defense
   c. Education
   d. Interest on the debt

4. The largest single category of outlays made by state and local governments is:
   a. national defense
   b. education
   c. highways
   d. public welfare

5. The benefits-received tax principle is best illustrated in the United States by:
   a. personal income taxes
   b. estate taxes
   c. payroll taxes
   d. fishing-license fees

6. Which of the following techniques would make good economic sense in determining how governmental expenditures could be rated according to their useful contribution to an economy?
   a. The number of people actually benefiting from the outlay
   b. Marginal social cost-marginal social benefit analysis
   c. The age of the recipients of the benefits
   d. The ability-to-pay principle

7. A value-added tax:
   a. evinces a semi-utilitarian attitude from its payers
   b. is imposed upon all stages of production
   c. is identical to a retail sales tax
   d. is imposed on the value added at each stage of production excluding the stage of final sale

8. An argument in favor of a progressive consumption tax is that:
   a. unlike personal income taxes, it doesn't tax savings
   b. it is more difficult for the government to spend the revenue from the tax
   c. people are unaware of it
   d. all of the above
   e. none of the above

9. The corporate income tax:
   a. is the largest revenue source for the federal government
   b. expired during the Obama administration
   c. is one where the statutory and economic incidences of the tax completely coincide
   d. all of the above
   e. none of the above

10. Which is not an argument posed by opponents of higher personal income tax rates?
    a. Taxes discourage savings
    b. Taxes that hit the well-to-do disproportionately hard are unfair
    c. A heavy tax rate on the rich sacrifices *equity* in favor of *efficiency*
    d. Heavy taxation destroys work incentives

11. When taxpayers' tax rates fall as their incomes rise, the tax in question is:
    a. a proportional tax
    b. a progressive tax
    c. a regressive tax
    d. all of the above
    e. none of the above

12. Which of the following is the best example of a proportional tax?
    a. A 7 percent sales tax
    b. A property tax
    c. A city's 1-percent gross income tax
    d. The federal personal income tax

13. Poverty rates in the United States reveal:
    a. that poverty rates tend to be lower for Asians versus other ethnic or racial groups
    b. equally distributed poverty rates across different demographic groups
    c. systematically lower rates for households headed by women
    d. that educational attainment has little impact upon the incidence of poverty

Use the diagram that follows to answer the next two questions.

14. The imposition of a tax will:
    a. move the supply curve from S to S_T
    b. move the supply curve from S_T to S
    c. increase output from Q_T to Q_E
    d. generate tax revenue of FGE

15. The deadweight loss from a tax can be represented by:
    a. the distance $P_T H$
    b. the triangle FGE
    c. the rectangle $TP_T HF$
    d. the trapezoid $FEQ_E Q_T$
    e. none of the above

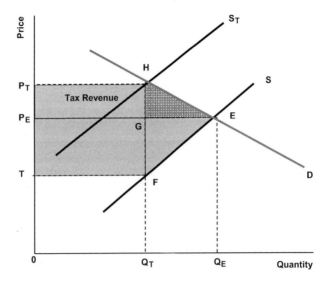

Problems and Thought Questions

1. Using the data in the table below, respond to the following questions.
   a. Complete the table by calculating the average and marginal tax rates.
   b. Taxes are regressive over what range of income?
   c. What range of income exhibits proportional tax rates?
   d. To what range of income are progressive tax rates applied?

Income	Taxes	Average Tax Rate (%)	Marginal Tax Rate (%)
$0	$0		
5,000	1,100		
10,000	2,100		
20,000	4,000		
25,000	5,000		
30,000	6,000		
35,000	7,000		
40,000	8,400		
50,000	11,500		
60,000	15,000		
70,000	18,900		
80,000	23,200		
90,000	27,900		
100,000	33,000		

2. Draw supply and demand curves to analyze and illustrate the following cases. Assuming the imposition of a unit excise tax, identify and explain the tax burden falling upon producer versus consumer. Indicate the revenue and excess burden in each case.
   a. Demand is relatively elastic compared to supply.
   b. Demand is relatively inelastic compared to supply.

ANSWERS TO SELF EXAMINATION

True/False

1. F
2. T
3. F
4. T
5. T
6. F
7. T
8. F
9. T
10. F
11. T
12. F
13. F
14. T
15. T

Multiple Choice

1. B
2. A
3. A
4. B
5. D
6. B
7. D
8. A
9. E
10. C
11. C
12. C
13. A
14. A
15. E

Problem and Thought Questions

1. a.

Income	Taxes	Average Tax Rate (%)	Marginal Tax Rate (%)
$0	$0		
5,000	1,100	22	22
10,000	2,100	21	20
20,000	4,000	20	19
25,000	5,000	20	20
30,000	6,000	20	20
35,000	7,000	20	20
40,000	8,400	21	28
50,000	11,500	23	31
60,000	15,000	25	35
70,000	18,900	27	39
80,000	23,200	29	43
90,000	27,900	31	47
100,000	33,000	33	51

b. $5,000 to $20,000
c. $20,000 to $35,000
d. $35,000 to $100,000

2. a. A relatively large cost in terms of deadweight loss (FHE) is conferred upon society to raise tax revenue TP_THF. The producers' burden is TP_E and the consumers' burden is P_EP_T.

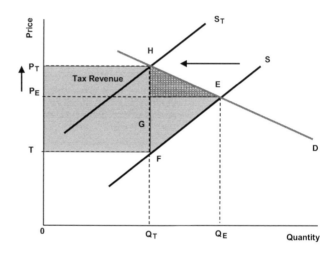

b. The bulk of the impact is to raise price. Consumers bear a larger share of tax burden compared to sellers. In this case, the excess burden (deadweight loss) of the tax is relatively small in relation to the revenue raised by the tax.

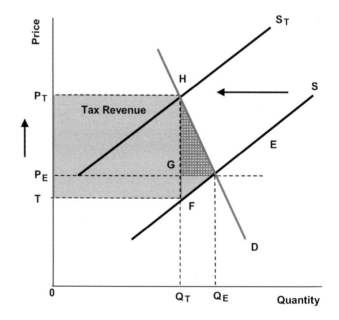

Part 3

Macroeconomics

Chapter 11

Accounting for Economic Fluctuations: Aggregate Demand and Aggregate Supply Analysis

KEY TERMS

Business cycle
Gross domestic product (GDP)
Aggregate demand
Personal consumption
  expenditures (C)
Gross private domestic
  investment (I_g)
Government purchases (G)
Net exports (X_n)
Nominal GDP

Real GDP
Aggregate supply
Real balances effect
Foreign purchases effect
Potential output (GDP)
Productivity
Demand-pull inflation
Multiplier
Cost-push inflation
Stagflation

CHAPTER SUMMARY

1. The principal focus of macroeconomics is three general measures of economic activity: the level of national output, the levels of employment and unemployment, and the price level. While microeconomics directed attention to the workings of individual markets, macroeconomics examines the aggregate performance of the economy.

2. The principal accounting measure of the aggregate output of the economy and the economy's overall performance is the gross domestic product (GDP). GDP is the market value of the goods and services produced in a country over a particular period. Other accounts used in measuring macroeconomic performance include gross national product, net national product, national income, personal income, and disposable personal income. Critical to comparing these measures over time is adjusting the dollar values for changes in the price level. By adjusting nominal GDP to a single base period, a measure of real GDP can be obtained to allow consistent comparisons between time periods. Chain-type indexes provide an improved method for adjusting and comparing real GDP figures and growth rates over time.

3. Levels of general business activity are subject to fluctuations, which are called business cycles. The

cyclical behavior of the economy has long attracted economists' attention and a variety of explanations have been put forward to explain the expansion and contraction of the economy. Indeed, the business cycle remains at the center of macroeconomic theory and policy-making objectives.

4. The principal tool of the modern-day macroeconomist in efforts to study and explain aggregate economic behavior is aggregate demand and aggregate supply analysis. By viewing aggregate output of the economy in terms of spending for goods and services (aggregate demand) and the output values of actual production (aggregate supply), the relationships that exist between price levels and levels of real output can be discerned. Shifts in aggregate demand and aggregate supply necessarily affect price level-output combinations. Examination of the factors contributing to such shifts supplies insights into the business-cycle phenomenon, allowing identification of which elements of an economy are the sources of economic expansion or the sources of contraction.

SELF EXAMINATION

True/False

1. The crash of 1929 was unlike any other business downturn because no economic signals were observable before the event to suggest that the economy was slipping into recession and contraction.
2. GDP counts transactions involving the purchase of financial instruments such as stocks and bonds but *not* interest and dividends.
3. The final value of all goods and services should equal the value added at all stages of the production of these goods.
4. The GDP measures *only* market transactions.
5. Government purchases do not contribute to national product.
6. A government transfer payment does not directly contribute to national output.

7. The expenditures side and the income side of the GDP account need not be equal.

8. Social security payments to individuals are not counted in GDP.

9. Personal savings is the difference between personal income and disposable income.

10. The difference between real GDP and nominal GDP is that nominal GDP measures output at current money levels.

11. Ordinarily we should expect rising prices at the contraction stage of the business cycle and rising unemployment during expansion.

12. Kondratieff's theory of cyclical trends posited long waves of forty to sixty years.

13. Firms tend to experience a rise in their excess capacity during the contraction and trough stages of the business cycle.

14. The Employment Act of 1946 mandated that government undertake policies that would maintain both stable prices *and* high levels of unemployment.

15. The real-balances effect is one of the reasons for aggregate demand to be a downward sloping curve.

16. A shift to the left in the aggregate supply curve has the effect of producing falling price levels and declining output.

17. GNP and GDP differ in that GDP excludes the profits made overseas by U.S. firms while GNP counts them.

18. GDP is widely regarded as a comprehensive and accurate measure of society's well-being.

Multiple Choice

1. Gross Domestic Product is:
   a. the sum of all sales of goods and services made in a single year
   b. the market value of all final goods and services produced over a particular period by a nation
   c. equal to all income received by the factors of production
   d. smaller than Net National Product

2. GDP:
   a. is arrived at by summing the price tags of all goods sold
   b. counts second-hand sales and resale
   c. measures only market transactions
   d. all of the above
   e. none of the above

3. Which of the following transactions will not be counted in GDP?
   a. Interest earned on a share of GM stock
   b. Rental income obtained by your landlord
   c. Social security payments to your grandparents
   d. The income of your dentist

4. The largest single entry on the expenditure side of American GDP is:
   a. personal consumption expenditures (C)
   b. gross private domestic investment (I)
   c. government purchases (G)
   d. net exports (X_n)

5. The largest entry on the income side of U.S. GDP accounts is:
   a. corporate profits
   b. corporate investment
   c. employee compensation
   d. government taxes

6. Which item must be added to national income in an effort to calculate personal income?
   a. Undistributed corporate profits
   b. Personal income taxes
   c. Government transfer payments to individuals
   d. Social-security contributions

7. Which of the following price indexes is based on a market basket of consumer goods?
   a. The GDP deflation
   b. The CPI
   c. The PPI
   d. The RPI

8. Which of the following is not likely to be a usual characteristic of the peak stage of the business cycle?
   a. High levels of employment
   b. Low unemployment
   c. High levels of investment
   d. High levels of consumer spending
   e. Falling prices

9. The economist most closely associated with the belief that long-term (fifty years) cyclical behavior was associated with invention or innovation is:
   a. William Stanley Jevons
   b. Robert Malthus
   c. Joseph Schumpeter
   d. Karl Marx
   e. J.M. Keynes

10. Which of the following is not true?
    a. $AD = C + I + G + X_n$
    b. $GDP = C + I + G + X_n$
    c. $C = I$
    d. X_n = Exports – Imports

11. The principle reason the AS curve rises as price levels rise is:
    a. in the short term profits rise when price levels rise
    b. the real balances effect
    c. the interest rate effect
    d. the multiplier effect

12. Which of the following will not tend to shift AS to the right?
    a. An increase in business taxes
    b. An increase in productivity
    c. An increase in profits
    d. A decline in labor costs

13. Keynesian economics:
    a. stressed the aggregate demand side of economic policy making
    b. is inherently inflationary
    c. pays too little attention to the economy's productive base
    d. all of the above
    e. none of the above

14. A rightward shift in the AD curve would be a likely result of:
    a. an increase in business investment
    b. a decline in the interest rate
    c. a decline in exports
    d. a rise in imports

15. Which shift will cause price levels to rise and output to fall?
    a. A leftward shift of AD
    b. A rightward shift of AS
    c. A rightward shift of AD
    d. A leftward shift of AS

Problems and Thought Questions

1. Given the following nominal GDP data and GDP implicit price deflator index data, convert the nominal GDP to real GDP.

Year	Nominal GDP	GDP Implicit Price Deflator Index (2005 = 100)	Real GDP
1930	91.1	10.2	
1945	223.0	11.08	
1975	1,637.7	33.56	
1995	7,414.7	81.53	
2005	12,638.4	100.0	

2. Answer the following questions using the aggregate supply diagram that follows.
    a. What does Y_p represent?
    b. Illustrate how aggregate demand might increase, raising output, but not price level.
    c. Illustrate how an increase in aggregate demand might increase both output price level.
    d. Illustrate how increasing aggregate demand increases only the price level.

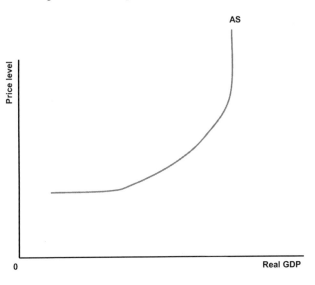

ANSWERS TO SELF EXAMINATION

True/False

1. F
2. F
3. T
4. T
5. F
6. T
7. T
8. T
9. F
10. T
11. F
12. T
13. T
14. F
15. T
16. F
17. T
18. F

Multiple Choice

1. B
2. A
3. C
4. A
5. C
6. C
7. B
8. E
9. C
10. C
11. A
12. A
13. A
14. A
15. D

Problem and Thought Questions

1. _____

Year	Real GDP
1930	$892.8
1945	2,012.4
1975	4,879.5
1995	9,093.7
2005	12,638.4

2. a. The potential output of the economy or full employment level of GDP.
   b. AD_1 to AD_2
   c. AD_2 to AD_3
   d. AD_4 to AD_5

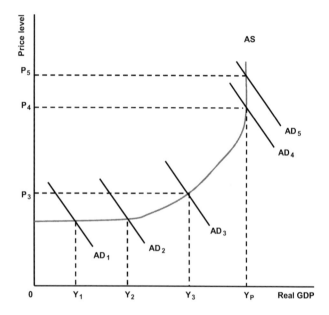

Chapter 12

Maintaining a Rising Level of Output: The Importance of Economic Growth

KEY TERMS

Economic growth

Technology

Technological progress

Real GDP per capita

Rule of 70

Potential real GDP

World Bank

Developing countries (DCs)

Malthusian principle

Vicious circle of poverty

Dual economies

Appropriate technology

Advanced industrial countries

CHAPTER SUMMARY

1. Economic growth can be depicted as an outward shift of the production-possibilities curve. Such a shift means that more output combinations are available. The principal ingredients of economic growth are labor force size and quality, capital stock size and quality, the rate of technological progress, the quality and amount of other resources, the efficiency of resource allocation, and the economy's aggregate demand for goods and services.

2. Authoritative growth accounting estimates reveal that increases in the quantity of labor accounted for 32 percent of the growth in real national income from 1929 to 1982. Increased labor productivity contributed to the remaining 68 percent that was attributable to technological advance (28 percent), quantity of capital (19 percent), education and training (14 percent), economies of scale (9 percent), and improved resource allocation (8 percent). The legal-human environment created a drag on labor productivity by subtracting from productivity growth from 1929 to 1982. The loss attributable to the legal-human institutional features might, however, be offset by certain gains in the quality of life manifested as improvement of the natural environment or safer working conditions.

3. Neoclassical growth theory divides the sources of productivity growth into capital deepening, increases

in skills, and efficiency gains. Efficiency gains dominate in importance during the period 1990–2005 in contributing to productivity growth while capital deepening and skills improvements made roughly constant contributions. Efficiency gains were more pronounced in sectors that made significant investments in information technology.

4. Conventional means of measuring economic growth include tracking changes in real GDP, real GDP per capita, and labor productivity. Real GDP was more than thirteen times larger in 2008 than in 1929. Living standards as measured by GDP per capita were five times higher in 2006 than in 1929. The long-term trend has been interrupted only by the major economic downturns.

5. The rule of 70 provides a means for quickly calculating the number of years it takes for output or living standards to double by dividing 70 by the percentage growth rate.

6. Sustaining economic growth is dependent upon macroeconomic stability and adaptation to structural changes in the economy. Historical experience suggests that technological change, labor force quality, capital formation, and management skill are important determinants of productivity growth. The economy's transition to a "knowledge-based economy" with heavy reliance upon services poses an economy of a different structure, which has entailed new experiences in productivity growth.

7. The population problem posited by Thomas Malthus in 1798 postulates that population growth will exceed growth in the food supply, thereby forcing living standards to the subsistence level. Advanced industrial countries have avoided the Malthusian prophecy through rising productivity and slower population growth. For many developing countries, the Malthusian scenario seems very real.

8. Separating countries according to industrial development is a conventional and convenient way of analyzing the circumstances that have produced high-income, middle-income, and low-income countries. The differences can be vast, with GDP per capita in advanced industrial countries far more than $11,000 while the lowest-income developing countries have GDP per capita below $200. World Bank data reveal that 84 percent of the world's population resides in low- or middle-income countries.

9. Generally, developing countries are caught in a cycle of lower development. High rates of population growth contribute to low GDP per capita. Low GDP per capita leads to low saving, which leads to low investment in human and physical capital. Low levels of investment depress productivity and total output. When this is coupled with population growth, low GDP per capita is the result. The stage is set for subsequent rounds of circular causation.

10. DCs are denied easy access to more rapid growth rates because of poor infrastructure, low investment, capital flight, unequal distribution of income, natural disasters, wars, and cultural-institutional features that are not conducive to economic development.

11. The key growth policies for the United States are generally encapsulated in sound aggregate demand-aggregate supply management. Narrowly focused policies include tax incentives for investment in capital goods and research and development, proposals to reform primary and secondary education, immigration reforms, infrastructure improvement, and advocacy of free trade.

12. Growth policies on a global scale are directed mainly at assisting DCs. Primary assistance is in the form of capital formation and infrastructure, fostering technology transfer, encouraging free trade, and financing economic development through grants and loans (largely from rich countries to poor). Financial assistance to DCs for economic development can come as direct grants and loans from multilateral organizations such as the World Bank and the Inter-American Development Bank.

SELF EXAMINATION

True/False

1. High productivity is among the causes of lesser development.
2. Persistent declines in real GDP per capita are symptomatic of declining living standards.
3. An economy that is close to full employment will likely grow less than economies that have some "slack" with high rates of unemployment.
4. An economy that sacrifices consumer goods in order to increase its output of capital goods is likely to grow faster than one that sacrifices capital goods to obtain consumer goods.
5. Less developed countries tend to invest more in human capital than advanced industrial countries.
6. The United States has the highest living standard in the world based upon real GDP per capita statistics.
7. Many experts believe that U.S. economic growth is slow because the country has had a lack of success with aggregate supply policies.
8. A point outside the production-possibilities curve can be attained only if economic growth occurs.
9. An inward (leftward) shift of the production-possibilities curve displays economic growth.
10. The Malthusian problem is that growth in food and fiber will outrun the growth in population.

Multiple Choice

Answer the next four questions based upon the following diagram.

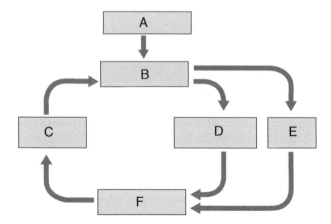

1. Box A should be labeled:
   a. low productivity and low total production
   b. low saving or low consumption and low level of aggregate demand
   c. low per-capita GDP
   d. high rate of population growth
   e. low investment in physical and human capital

2. Box B should be labeled:
   a. low productivity and low total production
   b. low saving or low consumption and low level of aggregate demand
   c. low per-capita GDP
   d. high rate of population growth
   e. low investment in real and human capital

3. Box F should be labeled:
   a. low productivity and low total production
   b. low saving or low consumption and low level of aggregate demand
   c. low per-capita GDP
   d. high rate of population growth
   e. low investment in real and human capital

4. Box C should be labeled:
   a. low productivity and low total production
   b. low saving or low consumption and low level of aggregate demand
   c. low per-capita GDP
   d. high rate of population growth
   e. low investment in real and human capital

5. Which of the following is the most likely source of a leftward shift of production-possibilities frontier for a developing country?
   a. Drought
   b. Large increases in the capital stock
   c. Exchange missionaries
   d. Rising educational levels

Answer the next three questions on the basis of the following diagrams:

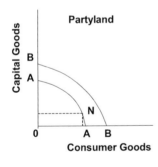
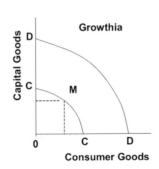

6. The country that exhibits the greatest economic growth is:
   a. Growthia with its shift from curve CC to DD
   b. Growthia with its shift from curve DD to CC
   c. Partyland with its shift from curve AA to BB
   d. not shown in either diagram

7. Which country has placed more emphasis on capital goods production?
   a. Partyland by choosing combination M
   b. Partyland by choosing N
   c. Growthia by choosing N
   d. Growthia by choosing M
   e. A country not shown in the diagram

8. If Partyland wanted greater growth in the future, what should it do in the present?
   a. Party on

b. Make a production choice similar to Growthia's point M
   c. Join a race to the bottom
   d. Stop producing consumer goods for a couple of years
   e. None of the above

9. Which of the following statements best describes the vicious circle of poverty in less-developed nations?
   a. High GDP per capita leads to high saving, investment, and consumption which raises productivity and lowers GDP per capita
   b. Low GDP per capita leads to low saving, investment, and consumption which results in low productivity and low GDP per capita
   c. They accumulate large debts with advanced countries then default and have to borrow more
   d. They trade low-value goods with other developing countries and end up with low-value goods

10. Supply-side policies to get the United States back on the faster growth track include:
    a. trade barriers
    b. getting the government "gravy-train" rolling again through more spending
    c. tax credits for investment and research and development
    d. electing an independent presidential candidate

11. Growth might be slowed by:
    a. war and droughts
    b. macroeconomic instability
    c. declining educational standards
    d. a productivity slowdown
    e. all of the above

12. The World Bank:
    a. makes loans available to developing countries to facilitate economic growth
    b. supplies currency to central banks throughout the world
    c. facilitates inter-planetary transactions
    d. gives away funds to poor countries

Problems and Thought Questions

1. Use a diagram to illustrate and explain the "vicious circle of poverty" experienced by many developing nations.
2. What are the supply and demand factors that are the "ingredients" of economic growth?
3. Use the production-possibilities curve model to show economic growth. Explain why your graph shows growth. What would have to happen in order for growth to occur?

ANSWERS TO SELF EXAMINATION

True/False

1. F
2. T
3. T
4. T
5. F
6. F
7. T
8. T
9. F
10. F

Multiple Choice

1. D
2. C
3. E
4. A
5. D
6. A
7. D
8. B
9. B
10. C
11. E
12. A

Chapter 13

Employment and Unemployment: Who Is Out of Work and Why?

KEY TERMS

Civilian labor force

Labor force participation rate

Unemployment

Full employment

Phillips curve

Rational expectations

Natural rate of
unemployment

Frictional unemployment

Structural unemployment

Cyclical unemployment

Adaptive expectations

CHAPTER SUMMARY

1. The economy's pool of available workers is drawn from the civilian noninstitutional population, age sixteen and older. Those individuals who are participating in the labor force are classified as employed or unemployed according to criteria applied by the Bureau of Labor Statistics. Roughly 65 percent of the civilian noninstitutional population, age sixteen and older, participates in the labor force. The labor force comprises more than 154 million people of whom, on average, 90.7 percent were employed and 9.3 percent were unemployed in 2009. Data for these measures come from the Current Population Survey of households. Another measure of employment is obtained from payroll data through the Current Employment Statistics Survey.

2. Unemployment is divided into three types: frictional, structural, and cyclical. Frictional unemployment arises when some workers enter or re-enter the labor force and others voluntarily leave jobs in search of new employment. Structural unemployment is associated with changes in the demand for labor caused by changing skill requirements, technological change, changes in the industrial composition of the economy, and changes in geographic patterns of employment. Cyclical unemployment is sensitive to changes in aggregate economic performance. Cyclical unemployment rises during economic downturns and falls during periods of prosperity.

3. The classical model of the labor market assumed wage flexibility that could be expected to guide the economy quickly back to full employment in the event of an excess supply of labor. Surplus labor would drive down wages, which would encourage employers to hire more labor at lower wages. Therefore, unemployment would be a temporary situation except for those who chose to be unemployed. John Maynard Keynes challenged the notion of wage flexibility and the economy's capacity to automatically gravitate to full employment. Written during the depths of the Great Depression, Keynes's *General Theory of Employment, Interest, and Money* became the intellectual foundation for the New Economics, which advocated government intervention to assure full employment.

4. The natural rate of unemployment is the rate of unemployment that would exist if the economy were operating at full capacity. The natural rate is the sum of frictional and structural unemployment.

5. Throughout the 1960s and into the 1970s, policymakers were fairly confident that full employment could be attained through government's manipulation of fiscal and monetary policy. However, policymakers were confronted with the dilemma of a tradeoff between unemployment and inflation, which is depicted by the Phillips curve.

6. The Phillips curve relationship broke down in the 1970s. Adaptive and rational expectations theorists argued that no stable Phillips curve relationship exists. Therefore, the economy tends to gravitate to its natural rate (or alternative variation, in the form of the nonaccelerating inflation rate of unemployment). These schools of thought question the effectiveness of discretionary policies to reduce unemployment below the natural rate.

7. The influence of expectations theories and doubts about effective implementation of fiscal policy have

led policymakers to deemphasize fiscal stabilization efforts in favor of monetary policy, which can be implemented quickly. Still, most economists and policymakers believe that fine-tuning the macroeconomy is probably an unrealistic goal for stabilization policy.

8. Structural unemployment develops differently in the Knowledge Economy than it did in the Industrial Age. Structural unemployment in the Industrial Age tended to be associated with obsolete skills caused by automation, but skills could often be adapted to new production, workers could reposition themselves on higher rungs on the occupational ladder, and the service sector became the dominant source of employment. The Knowledge Age economy's rapid technological advance combined with the forces of globalization expose both manufacturing and service employment to greater vulnerability than was perhaps the case in the Industrial Age.

9. A long history of government programs to deal with structural unemployment, training, and dislocated workers starts in significant magnitude at least as early as the 1930s, with the Federal Emergency Relief Administration, the Civilian Conservation Corps, and the Works Progress Administration. Various training and employment programs succeeded those of the Great Depression. The Workforce Investment Act of 1998 represented a major devolvement of work investment programs and activities to the state and local levels of government for implementation.

SELF EXAMINATION

True/False

1. The recession of 2007–2009 caused persistently high unemployment rates above 9 percent.
2. The civilian labor force is the sum of the number of employed and unemployed persons.
3. The civilian labor force participation rate is comparatively low by world standards.
4. "Full-employment" unemployment has historically been believed to be 2 to 3 percent unemployment.
5. The "natural rate of unemployment" is roughly the sum of frictional and structural unemployment.
6. Since the 1970s, we have seen the natural rate of unemployment continuously rise.
7. Cyclical unemployment trends higher during periods of economic prosperity.
8. Jobs lost due to machines replacing human labor are examples of cyclical unemployment.
9. Unemployment is a smaller problem, economically speaking, than it appears to be since work not done today can be done later without any social loss.

10. The Keynesian explanation of unemployment focused principally on the problem of insufficient demand for goods.
11. In the 1970s, we experienced a situation wherein aggregate demand expanded and produced "full employment" but at the cost of demand-pull inflation.
12. The high-water mark of the New Economics was reached during the Bush administration.
13. In the stagflationary 1970s, Americans discovered it was possible to have *both* high unemployment and high inflation.
14. The chronic stagflation of the 1970s was a direct challenge to, and ultimately the demise of, the New Economics.
15. Critics of "mismatch unemployment" maintain that inflexibly high wages are a major cause of structural joblessness.

Multiple Choice

1. Which of the following would disqualify an individual from being counted as part of the unemployed?
   a. Being on strike
   b. Having given up looking for work
   c. Absent from work due to illness
   d. All of the above
   e. None of the above

2. Involuntary unemployment refers to:
   a. all those who are out of work
   b. those who cannot find a wage that meets their expectations
   c. those who have been forced to retire due to age
   d. those workers ready, willing, and able to work who do not have jobs

3. The likely economic outcome of an effective minimum wage law would be to:
   a. increase the number of workers working
   b. raise all workers' wages or salaries
   c. reduce the number of unemployed
   d. all of the above
   e. none of the above

4. Which of the following might contribute to a rising natural rate of unemployment?
   a. Fewer young workers entering the labor force
   b. Increases in social-welfare spending by government
   c. The recent expansion of agricultural employment
   d. The way we count who is unemployed

5. The Wired Harness Corporation has moved all of its production operation to Iceland, and Gomez has

lost his job on the assembly line. His job loss is an example of:
a. frictional unemployment
b. structural unemployment
c. full employment unemployment
d. cyclical unemployment

6. Chronic inner-city unemployment among minority teenagers is an example of:
a. frictional unemployment
b. cyclical unemployment
c. structural unemployment
d. all of the above
e. none of the above

7. Efforts by government to stimulate the economy will have their most profound effect upon which of the following types of unemployment?
a. Cyclical
b. Frictional
c. Structural
d. International
e. Music industry

8. According to the Keynesian analysis, unemployment problems arise directly and indirectly as a result of:
a. excessive government spending
b. insufficient aggregate demand
c. demand-pull inflation
d. failures in aggregate supply

9. The "Great Society":
a. was a term coined by J.M. Keynes
b. was President Lyndon Johnson's name for his domestic economic program in the 1960s
c. sought to reduce both taxes and government spending to encourage economic growth
d. is best understood as yet another huge mistake committed by the baby-boom generation
e. none of the above

10. The first result of "too many dollars chasing too few goods" is:
a. price inflation
b. rising unemployment
c. a shortage of raw materials
d. supply shocks

11. Which of the following is not true about the American economy in the 1970s?
a. Supply shocks were pushing prices upward
b. Economic growth rates were well below our historical average
c. Unemployment rates were chronically high
d. All of the above
e. None of the above

12. Which of the following characterized the Reagan years?
a. Annually balanced budgets
b. A monetary policy experiment first introduced in the "Death Valley Days" television series
c. Continued stagflation
d. Continued high levels of inflation
e. Supply-side theory and policy

13. The Phillips curve:
a. posits a direct relationship between inflation and unemployment
b. is a cycle theory about unemployment
c. tracks the pace of hiring in the service sector
d. posits an inverse relationship between unemployment and inflation
e. was a baseball pitch so difficult to hit that many batters were sent to the unemployment line

14. "Adaptive expectations" asserts that:
a. citizens become so accustomed to government policy making that they ignore it
b. people just have to accept high unemployment rates during the Obama administration
c. people eventually learn the adverse consequences of government policies and react to protect their interests
d. government policy can routinely fool businesses and households into producing more through the use of inflationary stimuli

15. Rational expectations theory maintains:
a. people possess a rational understanding of the inflationary impact of expansionary government policies and take actions that nullify government's efforts to raise output
b. people rationally accept high unemployment rates during the Obama administration as the price of progress
c. people eventually learn the adverse consequences of government policies and react to protect their interests
d. government employs more rational people than average so that policy is above average as well

Problems and Thought Questions

1. Create a diagram to show the Phillips curve. Show how the curve might have changed positions from the 1960s forward. Relate the analysis to the natural rate of unemployment, adaptive expectations, and rational expectations.

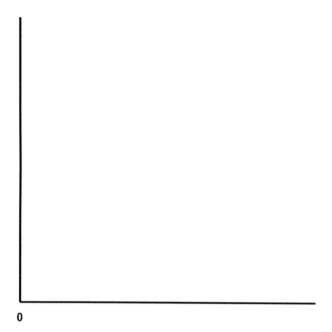

0

ANSWERS TO SELF EXAMINATION

True/False

1. T
2. T
3. T
4. F
5. T
6. F
7. F
8. F
9. F
10. T
11. T
12. F
13. T
14. T
15. T

Multiple Choice

1. D
2. D
3. E
4. B
5. B
6. C
7. A
8. B
9. B
10. A
11. E
12. E
13. D
14. C
15. A

Problems and Thought Questions

1.

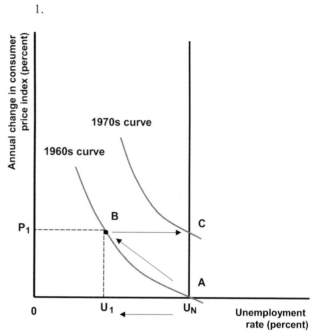

Chapter 14

The Federal Debt and Deficit Crisis: The Limits of Fiscal Policy

KEY TERMS

Budget deficit
Fiscal year
Debt
Employment Act of 1946
Automatic stabilizers
Fiscal drag

Structural deficit
Annually balanced budget
Cyclically balanced budget
Functional finance
Crowding-out effect

CHAPTER SUMMARY

1. The government experiences a budget deficit when expenditures exceed revenues in a fiscal year. A fiscal year is a budgetary planning period of any twelve consecutive months. The federal government's fiscal year is October 1 through September 30. The government accumulates debt when it runs deficits on a recurring basis.

2. The federal government has obligated itself to stabilize the economy. The principal reasons for deficits and the accumulation of debt are recession and war. The development of Keynesian economics during the Great Depression instilled a more active role for fiscal policy. Although deficits can function to stimulate a sagging economy, the tax reductions that create the stimulus have proven politically popular as well and have been utilized frequently in the post–World War II period, whether or not the economy needed them.

3. Keynesian theory emphasizes aggregate demand management, that is, the manipulation of taxes and government spending to achieve full employment. During the 1960s, Keynesian theorists argued that tax cuts could help bring the economy to full capacity. The demand-side stimulus worked but seemed to lose effectiveness in the 1970s, when inflation and "supply shocks" from the energy crisis confused policymakers about how to stabilize the economy. Overuse of deficit spending fueled inflation while producing little increase in output.

4. In practice, demand management theory is characterized not only by discretionary manipulation of taxes and spending but also by automatic stabilizers and an expansionary bias. The tax and transfer systems of the federal government are automatic stabilizers in the sense that recessions cause tax liabilities to fall and transfer expenditures to rise, while inflationary expansions bring rising incomes and tax liabilities while reducing claims to transfer payments.

5. Tax reductions in the 1980s were intended to stimulate the supply side of the economy, promote growth, and lower deficits. Instead, the lower tax structure and general rise in federal spending produced a large structural deficit. A structural deficit means that the budget will not balance even when the economy is operating at full employment. Structural deficits returned in 2002 after four years of budget surpluses.

6. Different philosophical perspectives on managing the federal budget include annually balanced budget, cyclically balanced budget, and functional finance. The annually balanced budget approach requires the budget to be balanced for each fiscal year. It is procyclical and impractical to implement under present circumstances. The cyclically balanced budget calls for balancing the budget over the business cycle. Asymmetry in economic expansions and downturns and political ambivalence have rendered this budget approach of little practical use. Finally, functional finance advocates stabilizing the economy without primary focus on the magnitude of deficits. The downside to this approach is that it can encourage fiscal irresponsibility and ignore the government's competing function of providing adequate levels of social goods.

7. Annual budget deficits have persisted since 1970, with the exception of 1998–2001. Deficits grew rapidly in the 1980s and the 2000s. Consequently, public debt now exceeds $12 trillion. These events and trends raise several issues about government finance: bankruptcy,

shifting burdens, crowding-out effect, trade deficits, inflation, redistribution of income, interest payments, and the weakening of fiscal policy effectiveness. In evaluating the importance of deficits and the attendant debt for the economic health of country, we are able to conclude that: (1) government bankruptcy is an unfounded concern; (2) shifting the debt burden to future generations is a controversial but minimal concern so long as we owe the debt to ourselves; (3) the crowding-out effect could subtly shift the burden of the debt by conferring a smaller capital stock upon future generations, but whether this actually occurs is unclear; (4) budget deficits can worsen the balance of trade, which impinges upon economic performance; (5) deficit spending can fuel inflation when the economy is at or close to full employment, but evidently this can be offset with restrictive monetary policy; (6) debt financing is probably increasing income inequality; (7) interest payments on the public debt are an increasing share of both the federal budget and GDP and indicate that debt financing is becoming an increasingly costly means of financing government functions; and (8) large deficits are symptomatic of low tax rates, comparatively high spending, and political ambivalence about responsible fiscal choices, so many observers wonder about the effectiveness of fiscal policy in the event of an economic crisis.

8. Public policy choices to deal with deficits and debt include a proposed constitutional amendment to balance the budget, budget baselines and caps, a line-item veto, privatization, capital budgeting, and requiring state and local governments to assume a greater share of fiscal responsibility. The constitutional amendment has been unable to gain necessary support for passage. The other approaches either lack adequate support or are unlikely to generate significant deficit reduction. Realistically, because a big portion of the annual deficit is structural in nature, the only way to reduce it is to reverse past discretionary tax-cutting and control spending.

9. The negative perception of government debt might distort thinking about how it can be used as a policy instrument to improve economic well-being. For example, a higher level of government debt is required in order to accomplish a welfare-enhancing transition from the existing Social Security system's "pay-as-you-go" method of financing to a saving-for-retirement system.

SELF EXAMINATION

True/False

1. The use of taxes and government spending to stabilize the economy is known as monetary policy.

2. During periods of prosperity, automatic stabilizers tend to cause a budget deficit.
3. Keynesian economics calls for budget deficits as a regular occurrence.
4. Keynesian economic theory tends to focus upon aggregate demand management.
5. If aggregate demand falls in the vertical range of the aggregate supply curve, both the price level and real output must fall.
6. The 2000s saw significant reductions in federal deficits and debt.
7. The only way to reduce government budget deficit is to raise taxes.
8. Substantial borrowing by the federal government might raise interest rates and thereby decrease private investment.
9. The structural deficit arises from cyclical changes in the economy.
10. Economists roundly agree that the burden of the federal debt is shifted to future generations.
11. Balanced budget amendments have been proposed over last three decades, but failed to pass in Congress.
12. Debt and deficit are interchangeable terms in the context of public finance.
13. The Employment Act of 1946 obligates the federal government to engage in stabilizing the economy.
14. A federal budget surplus in 2000 was short lived as subsequent wars and tax reductions bolstered a resumption of deficit spending.
15. Fiscal drag is associated with a structure of taxation that impedes economic growth.

Multiple Choice

1. One concern about running deficits every year is that:
    a. fiscal policy might be strengthened
    b. the government will go bankrupt
    c. the budget can never be balanced again
    d. fiscal policy has been weakened

2. The main reason that the federal government might incur surpluses or deficits is to:
    a. correct for spillover costs and benefits
    b. redistribute income to the rich
    c. stabilize the economy
    d. confuse the electorate

3. Which U.S. presidents were reluctant to lower taxes to stimulate the economy?
    a. Eisenhower and Truman
    b. Reagan and Carter
    c. Ford and Nixon
    d. Mulroney and Mitterand

4. Which of the following schools of thought emphasizes aggregate demand management over aggregate supply management?
   a. Reaganomics
   b. Supply-side economics
   c. Blind-side economics
   d. Keynesian economics
   e. Obamacare

5. Which of the following items are concerns about the public debt?
   a. The debt burden may be shifted to future generations
   b. The government has borrowed heavily from the Social Security system
   c. It can worsen the trade deficit
   d. All of the above

6. Attempting to balance the federal budget over a business cycle is the practice of:
   a. functional finance
   b. crowding out
   c. cyclically balancing the budget
   d. capital budgeting
   e. annually balancing the budget

7. If government deficits do raise interest rates, which in turn lowers investment spending, then:
   a. the budget will balance
   b. crowding out has occurred
   c. capital formation will necessarily increase
   d. the federal government must automatically default on its sovereign debt

8. If aggregate demand increases in the horizontal range of the aggregate supply curve:
   a. no change in real GDP will occur
   b. real GDP will rise, but not the price level
   c. real GDP and the price level will rise
   d. only the price level will rise

9. If aggregate demand increases in the upward sloping range of the aggregate supply curve:
   a. no change in real GDP will occur
   b. real GDP will rise, but not the price level
   c. real GDP and the price level will rise
   d. only the price level will rise

10. The notion of "twin deficits" refers to:
   a. the federal budget deficit causing a larger trade deficit
   b. both the federal government and the general public being heavily indebted
   c. having neither a bird in the hand nor one in the bush
   d. the coming crisis of the Social Security system

11. If aggregate demand increases in the vertical range of the aggregate supply curve:
   a. no change in nominal GDP will occur
   b. real GDP will rise, but not the price level
   c. real GDP and the price level will rise
   d. only the price level will rise

12. Fiscal policy in 2008 and 2009 can accurately be described as:
   a. reckless
   b. neutral
   c. focused exclusively on balancing the budget
   d. expansionary in an effort to counter the recession
   e. making the government the employer of first resort

Problems and Thought Questions

1. Compare and contrast the arguments against further accumulation of federal government debt versus in favor of greater debt. Explain precisely the rationale of each position.

2. Use diagrams to illustrate how the crowding-out effect could raise interest rates and reduce investment spending.

ANSWERS TO SELF EXAMINATION

True/False

1. F
2. F
3. F
4. T
5. F
6. F
7. F
8. T
9. F
10. F
11. T
12. F
13. T
14. T
15. T

Multiple Choice

1. D
2. C
3. A
4. D
5. D
6. C
7. B

8. B
9. C
10. A
11. D
12. D

Problems and Thought Questions

2.

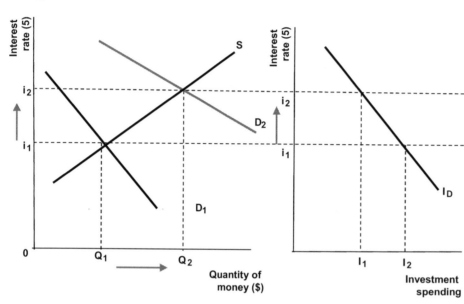

Chapter 15

Keeping Inflation Under Control:
The Limits of Monetary Policy

KEY TERMS

Inflation	Liquidity
Consumer price index	Multiple deposit creation
Producers price indexes	Fractional reserve system
GDP implicit price deflator	Required reserves
Personal consumption expenditures index	Excess reserves
	Money multiplier
Core inflation	Equation of exchange
Nominal income	Federal Reserve system
Real income	Open market operations
Demand-pull inflation	Reserve requirement
Cost-push inflation	Discount rate
Medium of exchange	Monetary rule
Standard of value	Incomes policies
Store of value	Indexation

CHAPTER SUMMARY

1. Inflation is a sustained increase in the general level of prices. The consumer price index (CPI) is most frequently used as a gauge of the price level. Calculating the percentage change in the CPI yields the inflation rate. Because the CPI is restricted to a market basket of goods and services, other measures of price levels, such as producer price indexes, the GDP implicit price deflator, and the personal consumption expenditures index (PCE), provide valuable multiple perspectives on prices and trends in inflation trends. Many economists and policymakers regard the PCE as a more comprehensive and a better source of information about the price level and inflation. Likewise, knowledgeable sources prefer to distinguish between "headline inflation" and core inflation, which excludes the volatile components of food and energy.

2. Consumer prices began a rapid trend upward in the 1960s. Inflation rates have varied widely in response to oil shocks, macroeconomic policies, and recession.

3. Inflation diminishes purchasing, arbitrarily redistributes income and wealth, increases nominal interest rates, adversely affects employment and output, and worsens the country's international position. Therefore, a macroeconomic policy goal is to keep inflation at a low level.

4. Demand-pull inflation occurs when aggregate demand increases at a rate that exceeds the rate of response in the economy's production capacity. The result is for prices to be bid up by the phenomenon of too much money chasing too few goods. Cost-push inflation occurs when rising production costs translate into higher prices.

5. Money is a medium of exchange, a standard value, and a store of value. Money is used in exchange primarily because of its acceptability. Measures of the money stock are based upon broadening definitions of liquid assets ranging from M1 (chiefly cash and checking accounts) and M2 (which includes less-liquid "near-monies").

6. The fractional reserve system allows depository institutions to create money by lending their excess reserves. A system of depository institutions can create a multiple expansion of deposits. The maximum expansion possible with a given level of excess reserves is expressed by the following formula: $D = E (1/r)$. The simple money multiplier is: $M_d = 1/r$.

7. The quantity theory of money relies upon the equation of exchange: $MV = PQ$ or $MV = GDP$. Assuming a constant velocity of money, the quantity theory predicts a direct, proportional relationship between money and nominal GDP. Since quantity theorists posit that the economy will tend to operate at full employment (Q constant). The rate of change in the money supply will determine the rate of change in the price level.

8. The Federal Reserve is the central bank of the United

States. Its most significant economic role is managing the supply of money. The Fed can stimulate economic activity by pursuing an easy money policy of buying securities on the open market, lowering the discount, and lowering reserve requirements. A tight money policy to fight inflation can be executed through the sale of securities on the open market, raising the discount rate, and raising reserve requirements. In practice, conducting open market operations is the most active tool of monetary policy.

9. Fed policy has been eclectic about the choice of monetary targets. Sometimes the Fed emphasizes interest rate targeting to stabilize or encourage borrowing and spending. At other times it attempts to control monetary aggregates to stop inflation.

10. Regulatory and institutional changes produced fluctuations in monetary aggregates, making them less dependable as policy targets and necessitating several redefinitions of these measures of the money supply. In recent years, wars, financial upheaval, and recession have added to the difficulty of balancing multiple objectives through monetary policy. The Fed added new monetary policy tools to respond to the liquidity problems of the financial system and a worldwide economic crisis that began in 2008.

11. Demand-pull inflation can be countered with restrictive fiscal and monetary policies, but the primary role has been relegated to monetary policy. A tight money policy can push down aggregate demand and the price level. The Fed has to be careful not to tighten too much and cause a severe recession.

12. Cost-push inflation can be countered with a persistent tight-money policy, but the result is almost inevitably a serious recession. This is because major episodes of cost-push inflation were produced by external shocks (oil crises and war), not by excessive aggregate demand.

13. Wage and price controls, incomes policies, and indexation are various means of combating or coping with inflation. The majority of economists would probably agree that such policies are no substitute for responsible and credible fiscal and monetary policies.

SELF EXAMINATION

True/False

1. Money functions as a medium of exchange, a store of value, and a standard of value.
2. The most liquid asset in the economy is a U.S. Savings Bond.
3. At full employment, an increase in the money supply with velocity constant will increase both P and Q in the equation of exchange.
4. Central supervision of the Federal Reserve System resides with the president of the United States and the Congress.
5. All depository institutions are required to be members of the Federal Reserve System.
6. The Federal Reserve Banks are owned by the people of the United States.
7. The simple money multiplier is the reciprocal of the reserve ratio.
8. Inflation is ordinarily thought of as a rapid increase in the price of one product.
9. The difference between nominal and real income is the reserve requirement.
10. Inflation can cause inefficiency and redistribute income.
11. During most periods of inflation, an easy-money policy is most appropriate.
12. Cost-push inflation is caused by too much aggregate demand.

Multiple Choice

1. Cost-push inflation is caused by:
   a. deficient aggregate demand
   b. excessive aggregate demand
   c. declining aggregate supply
   d. an easy-money policy

2. Real income differs from nominal income in that:
   a. real income is less important
   b. real income measures current money income while nominal income measures the physical amount of goods and services that a given money income can purchase
   c. real income is computed with respect to base-period prices while nominal income is stated in current prices
   d. low-income people have no measurable real income

3. If the simple money multiplier is 4, then the reserve requirement must be:
   a. 25 percent
   b. 20 percent
   c. slightly above 75 percent
   d. 80 percent
   e. impossible to calculate

4. The expression MV = PQ is:
   a. the equation for the simple money multiplier
   b. a method of calculating the velocity of a falling object dropped from the top of the New York Federal Reserve Bank

c. the equation for calculating the consumer price index

d. the monetarist equation of exchange

e. the incomes policy index

5. Anticipated inflation:
   a. raises nominal interest rates
   b. lowers nominal interest rates
   c. leaves economic behavior unchanged
   d. makes people feel good about the future

6. Which of the following formulas should be used to calculate the inflation rate between 2010 and 2009?

   a. $\frac{CPI2010 - CPI2009}{CPI2010} \times 100$

   b. $\frac{CPI2010}{CPI2010 - CPI2009} \times 100$

   c. $\frac{CPI2010 - CPI2009}{CPI2009} \times 100$

   d. $\frac{CPI2010 - CPI2009}{CPI\ base\ period} \times 100$

7. A system of depository institutions with excess reserves of $17,000 and a reserve ratio of 1/3 can expand the money supply by:
   a. $5,100
   b. $15,300
   c. $51,000
   d. $17,000
   e. zero, a banking system cannot be used to increase or decrease the money supply

8. A supply-side anti-inflation policy would emphasize tax reductions and relaxation of certain regulations to:
   a. increase aggregate supply and raise real GDP
   b. increase aggregate demand and raise real GDP
   c. increase aggregate supply, but reduce real GDP
   d. increase both aggregate supply and aggregate demand equally, thus stabilizing prices and raising real GDP

9. Relying upon the equation of exchange, an unstable velocity of money has the effect of:
   a. making monetary policy more reliable
   b. making monetary policy more difficult to formulate and enact
   c. stabilizing the economy
   d. hampering price controls

10. The Federal Reserve's monetary policy during the period of the "Great Recession" from 2007–2009 can be categorized as:
    a. an easy-money policy oriented toward fighting recession and stimulating growth
    b. a neutral monetary policy of "allowing the chips to fall where they may"
    c. a tight-money policy designed to fight recession and stimulate growth
    d. a supply-side tax cut

11. If monetary authorities apply a "Taylor rule":
    a. an unchanging rate of growth in the money supply would be adopted
    b. short-term interest rates are manipulated to meet a long-run inflation target that is consistent with full employment
    c. a series of monetary shocks are delivered to the economy to either speed it up or slow it down
    d. the Federal Open Market Committee would as a rule always consult with economist John Taylor before implementing changes to monetary policy

12. Among the shortcomings that have been ascribed to the consumer price index is:
    a. it could fail to account for consumers substituting cheaper goods for more expensive ones
    b. it doesn't capture improvements in product quality
    c. it is limited to a "basket" of consumer goods
    d. all of the above

Problems and Thought Questions

1. Use the aggregate supply-aggregate demand model to demonstrate cost-push inflation.

2. Explain how the reserve requirement affects the size of the money multiplier.

3. Explain how the Federal Reserve can use the three quantitative tools of monetary policy to pursue:
   a. an easy-money policy
   b. a tight-money policy

4. List and explain the consequences of inflation. How do these consequences influence policies that you would propose to deal with inflation?

5. Trace the following transactions with the use of T-accounts:
   a. $75,000 is deposited in a checking account at Megabank and the reserve requirement is 7 percent.
   b. The bank lends all of its excess reserves by way of a loan-created demand deposit.
   c. Excess reserves are paid out to cover the loan.

6. Calculate the money multiplier given the following reserve ratios:
   a. 100 percent
   b. 50 percent
   c. 25 percent
   d. 10 percent
   e. 0 percent

ANSWERS TO SELF EXAMINATION

True/False

1. T
2. F
3. F
4. F
5. F
6. F
7. T
8. F
9. F
10. T
11. F
12. F

Multiple Choice

1. C
2. C
3. A
4. D
5. A
6. D
7. C
8. A
9. B
10. A
11. B
12. D

Problems and Thought Questions

1.

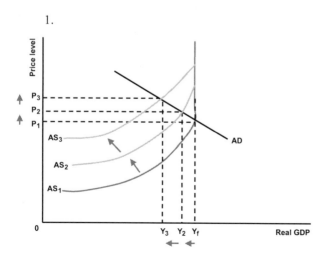

2. There is an inverse relationship between the reserve requirement and the money multiplier.

3. a. Lower reserve requirements, lower discount rate, buy securities in the open market, lower interest rates on required and excess reserve balances, make fewer term deposits available
   b. Raise reserve requirements, raise discount rate, sell securities in the open market, increase interest rates on required and excess reserve balances, make more term deposits available

5. a.

Assets	Liabilities
Reserves: $75,000	Demand Deposits $75,000

b.

Assets	Liabilities
Reserves: $75,000	Demand Deposits $144,750
Loans: $69,750	

c.

Assets	Liabilities
Reserves: $5,250	Demand Deposits $75,000
Loans: $69,750	

6. a. 1
   b. 2
   c. 4
   d. 10
   e. ∞

Part IV

International Economics

Chapter 16

America in the World: International Trade

KEY TERMS

Comparative advantage
Autarky
Trading possibilities curve
Protectionism
Tariff
Revenue tariffs
Protective tariffs
Import quota

Voluntary restraint agreements
Dumping
Infant industries argument
Breathing room argument
National defense argument
Industrial policy
World Trade Organization
Foreign direct investment

CHAPTER SUMMARY

1. International economic interdependence is pushing regions toward economic integration. The North American Free Trade Agreement (NAFTA) established a free trade zone in North America. This has been followed by a raft of free trade agreements around the globe.

2. The principle of comparative advantage states that if countries specialize in goods that they can produce at a lower relative opportunity cost and then trade, the world's scarce resources will be used efficiently and all countries can attain higher living standards. The predicted results from the application of the principle of comparative advantage make a strong economic argument in favor of free trade.

3. Protectionism refers to the practice of shielding domestic industries from foreign competition. Trade barriers include (a) tariffs—excise taxes on imported goods; (b) import quotas—restrictions on the number of units permitted for import; (c) voluntary export restrictions or voluntary restraint agreements, in which the exporting country agrees to limit the physical number of goods exported; and (d) regulatory barriers consisting of licensing requirements, codes, standards, bureaucratic procedures, and other technical barriers to trade (TBTs).

4. Trade barriers are rationalized on the basis of (a) a response to the dumping of foreign goods on the domestic market, (b) protecting "infant industries," (c) provision of "breathing room" for decrepit industries, (d) ensuring national security, (e) rectifying trade imbalances, and (f) pursuing industrial policy strategies. Generally speaking, none of these arguments dissuade economists from the position that free trade is the best trade policy.

5. The World Trade Organization (WTO) has a membership of 153 countries. The WTO's key purpose is multilateral reductions in trade barriers. The WTO advances five basic principles: (1) nondiscrimination—each member country must offer all other WTO members the most favorable treatment supplied to any country, (2) freer trade through negotiation, (3) predictability through binding and transparency, (4) promoting fair competition, and (5) encouraging development and economic reform. Several "rounds" of trade negotiations have been undertaken since creation of the General Agreement on Tariffs and Trade (GATT) and its successor, the WTO, in an effort to increase the scope of multilateral trade liberalization.

6. The United States has maintained its commitment to multilateral trade liberalization, but in the early 1990s began to pursue more bilateral free trade agreements (FTAs) and regional trade agreements (RTAs). As of the beginning of 2010, seventeen FTAs were in force. Most favored nation (MFN) clauses in FTAs or RTAs would help prevent trade-distorting impacts from adding to the proliferation of bilateral trade agreements.

7. The question of whether freer trade increases trade is not settled. However, the evidence indicates that the GATT did substantially increase trade among participating countries regardless of whether they were formal members.

8. Policies for improving the U.S. balance of trade include credible fiscal and monetary policies, reducing the budget deficit, encouraging economic growth abroad, encouraging free trade, and initiatives leading to a more competitive economic environment that makes better products for consumption domestically or for export.

SELF EXAMINATION

True/False

1. Higher domestic income levels generally cause imports to rise.
2. Protectionism is the practice of shielding domestic industries from international competition.
3. The General Agreement on Tariffs and Trade was designed to lower trade barriers among as many trading nations as possible.
4. One good thing about U.S. restrictions on imports is that they have really saved U.S. jobs.
5. A comparative advantage exists when a country can produce a product at a lower absolute cost.
6. Industrial policy would seek a comprehensive government-business strategy to improve export growth.
7. The role of GATT was subsumed by the creation of the World Trade Organization.
8. Technical trade barriers are associated with unnecessarily cumbersome regulations and licensing arrangements that restrict trade.
9. Empirical research conclusively states that successful completion of the Doha Round of trade negotiations will generate no economic gain.
10. Bilateral trade agreements involve agreements of just about every nation, while multilateral trade agreements are between just two countries.

Multiple Choice

Answer the next three questions using the following diagram:

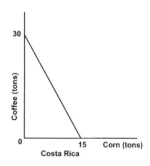

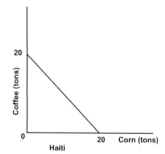

1. Which country has the comparative advantage in the production of coffee?
   a. Costa Rica

   b. Haiti
   c. Neither possesses a comparative advantage in coffee production
   d. Both possess a comparative advantage in coffee production

2. According to information provided:
   a. Haiti should specialize in and import corn
   b. Haiti should specialize in and export coffee
   c. Costa Rica should specialize in and export coffee
   d. Costa Rica will be better off without trade

3. If the actual terms of trade between the two countries were that 1 ton of corn is exchanged for 1 1/2 tons of coffee, which of the following statements would be correct with respect to complete specialization and trade?
   a. Haiti's trading possibilities curve will be anchored at 45 tons of coffee
   b. Costa Rica's trading possibilities curve will be anchored at 45 tons of corn
   c. Haiti's trading possibilities curve will be located at 30 tons of coffee
   d. People in Haiti will have to drink a lot less coffee

4. An excise tax placed upon an imported product is commonly called:
   a. a tariff
   b. a quota
   c. an embargo
   d. an import license

5. Which of the following arguments are consistent with erecting trade barriers to protect domestic industries?
   a. Infant industries
   b. National defense
   c. Breathing room
   d. Protect American jobs
   e. All of the above

Answer the next six questions using the following diagram:

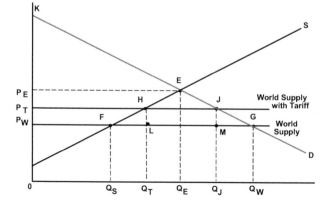

6. In a tariff-free environment and a world supply of the product as shown:
   a. domestic producers would supply $0Q_S$ and Q_SQ_W will be supplied by the rest of the world
   b. domestic producers would supply $0Q_E$ and Q_EQ_W will be supplied by the rest of the world
   c. domestic producers would supply Q_SQ_W and $0Q_S$ will be supplied by the rest of the world
   d. $0Q_E$ will be supplied, divided equally between domestic and foreigner suppliers in order to be fair

7. If a tariff is imposed as shown:
   a. domestic suppliers gain FHL
   b. domestic suppliers lose JMG
   c. domestic suppliers gain P_WP_THF
   d. domestic consumers gain Q_JQ_WGJ
   e. domestic consumers gain Q_JQ_WGM

8. If a tariff is imposed as shown:
   a. the revenue going to the government is LHJM
   b. the revenue going to the government is FHJM
   c. the revenue going to the government is Q_TQ_JJH
   d. no revenue is raised by the tariff

9. Moving from autarky to free trade:
   a. is bad economic policy
   b. causes domestic suppliers to contract output by Q_SQ_T
   c. causes domestic suppliers to contract output by Q_SQ_W
   d. enlarges consumer surplus by FHL
   e. causes domestic suppliers to contract output by Q_SQ_E

10. Moving from autarky to free trade:
    a. enlarges consumer surplus by P_WP_EEG
    b. leaves consumer surplus unaffected
    c. should go slow by imposing a tariff of P_T first
    d. results in a loss of consumer surplus

11. If the government resorts to a quota of Q_TQ_J:
    a. the effect is identical to that of the tariff shown in the diagram
    b. society will be safer by buying fewer foreign-made goods
    c. technical barriers to trade are definitely involved
    d. the government forgoes revenue of LHJM, which is realized as a gain by foreign sellers

12. Which of the following alternatives is the best for reestablishing higher levels of U.S. exports?
    a. Slap tariffs on everything in which the United States lacks a comparative advantage
    b. Treat all U.S. industries as infants
    c. Become more competitive and produce better products
    d. Regard more industries as essential to national defense and security

Problems and Thought Questions

1. Discuss multilateral efforts to reduce trade barriers. How do trading blocs reduce some trade barriers while erecting others?
2. Graph the following production-possibilities data for the United States and Nigeria. Identify their respective comparative advantages. Graph the trading-possibilities curve of each country if the terms of trade are 1 oil can be exchanged for 1 1/4 steel.

U.S.		Nigeria	
Oil	Steel	Oil	Steel
0	18	0	3
3	12	2	2
9	6	4	1
12	0	6	0

ANSWERS TO SELF EXAMINATION

True/False

1. T
2. T
3. T
4. F
5. F
6. T
7. T
8. T
9. F
10. F

Multiple Choice

1. A
2. C
3. B
4. A
5. E
6. A
7. C
8. A
9. E
10. A
11. D
12. C

Problems and Thought Questions

2. The cost ratios are: U.S.: 2 steel = 1 oil; Nigeria: 1 steel = 2 oil. Thus, the United States has the comparative advantage in steel and Nigeria has the comparative advantage in oil. Specialization and trade will anchor the U.S. trading-possibilities curve at 18 steel and 14.4 oil. Nigeria's curve will be anchored at 6 oil and 7.5 steel.

Chapter 17

America in the World: International Finance

KEY TERMS

Exchange rate
Floating exchange rate
Currency appreciation
Currency depreciation
Balance of payments
Current account

Balance of trade
Balance on income
Balance of current account
Capital account
Financial account

CHAPTER SUMMARY

1. The need to finance international trade gives rise to the existence of foreign exchange markets, where currencies are swapped to settle international payments. Exchange rates between currencies are, for most countries, floating; that is, they are determined by the forces of supply and demand. Appreciation means that a currency's price in terms of other currencies has risen. Depreciation means that a currency's price in terms of other currencies has declined. Currency appreciation makes imports cheaper; it increases imports and decreases exports. Currency depreciation makes foreign goods more expensive, thereby decreasing imports and encouraging exports.

2. The economic variables that determine a currency's exchange rate include (a) growth in real GDP, (b) the change in relative prices between trading partners, (c) changes in demand for domestic versus foreign goods, (d) relative real interest rates between trading partners, and (e) the effects of economic expectations and currency speculation.

3. The Bretton Woods system of fixed exchange rates dominated trade from 1945 until 1971. The U.S. suspension of fixed convertibility of dollars for gold signaled the demise of fixed exchange rates. Thereafter, major industrialized countries have resorted to a "managed float."

4. The balance of payments is a summary of payments between trading partners. The payments are allocated to the current account, the capital account, or the financial account.

5. The balance of trade refers to the net of goods and services exports minus goods and services imports. The U.S. trade balance has been negative since 1976. Persistent imbalances have made the United States a debtor country. In other words, the United States owes more to the rest of the world for the goods and services from abroad that it has consumed than it is owed by the rest of the world. The United States finances its balance of payments deficit largely through borrowing from foreign countries; this appears as an inflow on the capital account or financial account.

6. Fixed exchange rates have the advantage of reducing the risk and uncertainty associated with import-export transactions, but foreign exchange markets and the coordinated government intervention has offset risk and uncertainty. Floating exchange rates have the advantage of automatically correcting for balance of payments deficits and surpluses.

7. U.S. intervention in foreign exchange markets has been limited and infrequent over the past decade.

SELF EXAMINATION

True/False

1. President Nixon enacted the gold standard for international trade in August 1971.
2. When real interest rates are relatively high in a country, the country tends to experience a capital inflow.
3. A weaker dollar corresponds with higher import prices.
4. Direct foreign investment in the United States tends to improve the overall balance of payments.
5. An exchange rate is the number of units of a currency required to purchase a unit of foreign currency.

6. Floating exchange rates mean that currency values are established by government decree.

7. A currency appreciates when its value falls relative to other currencies.

8. A currency depreciates when its value falls relative to other currencies.

9. The Bretton Woods Agreement called for fixed exchange rates after World War II.

10. Uncertainty and risk in international transactions is one of the inherent problems with floating exchange rates.

Multiple Choice

1. Flexible exchange rates mean that:
   a. a currency trades for a fixed number of units of another currency
   b. currency exchange rates fluctuate according to demand and supply in the foreign exchange market
   c. all countries' currencies are pegged to gold
   d. governments require convergence to a narrow band of exchange rates

2. A "trade deficit" typically refers to:
   a. an excess of capital inflows over outflows
   b. less government revenue than spending
   c. an excess of merchandise and services imports over merchandise and services exports
   d. a macroeconomic automatic stabilizer
   e. the so-called "brain drain" of skilled workers from less-developed countries

3. In a regime of flexible exchange rates, an increase in the demand for dollars relative to the euro would mean that
   a. more euros are required to buy the dollar
   b. fewer euros are required to buy the dollar
   c. more dollars are required to buy the euro
   d. the euro will appreciate

4. Generally speaking, stronger growth in the United States will:
   a. have no effect on the exchange rate for the dollar
   b. cause the dollar to depreciate
   c. raise tariffs
   d. cause the dollar to appreciate

5. In recent years the Federal Reserve:
   a. has regularly intervened in foreign exchange markets at the direction of the U.S. Treasury
   b. typically has not intervened in foreign exchange markets
   c. was expressly prohibited from intervening in foreign exchange markets by the amendment of the Federal Reserve Act

   d. was still trying to learn how it could intervene in foreign exchange markets

6. The balance of payments:
   a. equals real GDP
   b. is divided into the expenditures account and the income account
   c. is the difference between merchandise exports and imports
   d. is an accounting statement of payments made and payments received between one country and other countries

7. The "dark matter" proposition:
   a. is used to explain the U.S. deficit in income in the balance of payments while having a negative net international investment position
   b. suggests that the U.S. exports inferior managerial knowhow, which bolsters income flows in return to the United States
   c. states that greater returns are earned on assets abroad
   d. is used to explain the U.S. surplus in income in the balance of payments while having a negative net international investment position

8. Which of the following is a determinant of a currency's exchange rate?
   a. Growth in real GDP
   b. The change in relative prices between trading partners
   c. Changes in demand for domestic versus foreign goods
   d. Relative real interest rates between trading partners
   e. All of the above

9. Currency forward, futures, and options contracts:
   a. evolved because of the need to hedge against fluctuating exchange rates
   b. ceased to be used after fixed exchange rates were abandoned
   c. were developed by currency speculators for the sole purpose of establishing the means for currency traders and brokers to get rich
   d. none of the above

10. Which of the following statement is true?
   a. The United States has run a current account deficit since the early 1990s
   b. The United States has run a negative balance in goods and services since the early 1990s
   c. The United States has run a positive balance on income for several decades
   d. all of the above
   e. none of the above

Problems and Thought Questions

1. Given the following data, make the appropriate calculations to answer the questions below (figures are in millions of dollars).

Exports of goods and services	$1,643,168
Imports of goods and services	2,344,590
Income receipts	818,931
Income payments	728,085
Unilateral net transfers	115,996
Net capital account transactions	1,895
U.S.-owned assets abroad, excluding financial derivatives	1,472,126
Foreign-owned assets in the United States, excluding financial derivatives	2,129,460
Net financial derivatives	6,222

a. What is the balance on goods and services?
b. What is the current account balance?
c. What is the balance on income?
d. What is the balance on goods, services and income?

2. Use a diagram of the supply and demand for dollars to show the appreciation or depreciation of the dollar under the following circumstances:
a. the demand for dollars rises
b. the demand for dollars falls
c. the supply of dollars decreases
d. the supply of dollars increases

ANSWERS TO SELF EXAMINATION

True/False

1. F
2. T
3. T
4. T
5. T
6. F
7. F
8. T
9. T
10. T

Multiple Choice

1. B
2. C
3. A
4. D
5. B
6. D
7. D
8. E
9. A
10. D

Problems and Thought Questions

1. $
   a. −701,422
   b. −494,580
   c.   90,846
   d. −610,576

2.
   a. appreciates
   b. depreciates
   c. appreciates
   d. depreciates